Bobbin Lace Braid

Gilian Dye

Bobbin Lace Braid

B.T. Batsford Ltd   London

ISBN 0 7134 1594 0

Filmset in 'Monophoto' Sabon by
Servis Filmsetting Limited, Manchester

Printed by The Anchor Press Ltd, Tiptree, Essex
for the publishers B.T. Batsford Limited
4 Fitzhardinge Street, London W1H 0AH

Contents

Introduction 7

1   Equipment 9
2   Basic Techniques 13
3   Basic Braid and its Variations 22
4   Straight Braids 34
5   Curves and Angles 51
6   Patterned Braids and Edgings 59
7   Torchon Lace 75
8   Additional Techniques 87
9   Trimmings, Motifs and Accessories 98

Abbreviations 130
Glossary 131
Appendix 132
Suppliers of Equipment and Materials 134
Bibliography 136
Index 139

Introduction

As soon as man had time to spare from the task of survival he began to decorate the things around him. Braids, at first merely functional, became a common form of decoration on clothing, furnishings, harness, etc, and have remained popular over many centuries.

Many methods have been used in the making of these braids. Twisting together two or more threads was probably the earliest technique; later plaiting, knotting and weaving became more important. By the end of the fifteenth century a craft had been developed that combined something of all these techniques. This was the craft of Bobbin Lace (sometimes called Pillow Lace). It reached its zenith in the sixteenth and seventeenth centuries when magnificent lace was produced, often in elaborate designs and some from linen thread no thicker than a hair. Each thread was wound on a bobbin which then acted as a handle while the threads were twisted and interwoven into the required pattern. Since some of the more detailed designs required a thousand threads, or more, the handling of all those bobbins was obviously only for the expert. However, the same techniques, with relatively few bobbins, may be used by the amateur to create a wide variety of attractive braids from the wealth of threads available today.

Braids made by this method can be used in many ways. The compact braids when worked by the metre or yard may be applied like any commercially produced braid; others, more open and 'lacy', are suitable for edgings or insertions. The great advantage of using bobbins is, however, that the braids can be shaped as they are worked – into simple neat corners, or quite complex fabrics or motifs.

This book, although planned for the complete beginner to lacemaking, will, I hope, offer some new ideas to the more experienced worker. It explains the simpler lace techniques and shows how they may be used in various combinations to give unusual and decorative effects. No attempt has been made to cover the traditional forms of fine lace, but the Bibliography at the end of this book contains a short list of publications in which these are described.

The first chapter deals with the equipment required: the tools, like the techniques, are those of the lacemaker and instructions are given for making the modern equivalents of the old (and now scarce and expensive) bobbins and pillows. Chapter 2 describes the basic techniques for using this equipment, while in the following chapters other techniques are explained as they are required for working the various examples. Chapters 3, 4, 6 and 7 contain instructions for straight braids. Simple shaping methods are given in chapter 5, with further information in chapter 8. The final chapter demonstrates a selection of the almost unlimited variety of useful and decorative items that may be created. Further information on equipment, materials (including a list of suppliers) and lacemaking classes is given at the end of the book.

I would like to thank the many people who have helped – either directly, or indirectly – in compiling this book. I offer particular thanks to my teacher, Mrs J. Minns, who has borne my experiments with patience and given much help and advice; to Gerard Parkinson who took the photographs; and to my family who have come to accept, if not to enjoy, a house full of pins and the clicking of bobbins.

7

1 Equipment

The pillow

A smooth, firm surface is needed on which to work the braids. This can be simply a sheet of fibre insulating board (preferably covered with fabric), but a tightly packed 'pillow' is an easier base on which to work. The pillow must take pins readily and hold them firmly in position.

Two types of pillow are described here. The cylindrical pillow is most suitable for working long lengths, the flat pillow is better for shaped pieces. Since the first patterns are all for straight braids the preliminary instructions are given for working on a cylindrical pillow. See the notes in chapter 2 for working on a board or flat pillow.

To make a simple cylindrical pillow
Fill a tin can or similar container (eg a small drinking-chocolate tin) with pebbles (for weight) and sawdust (to prevent rattling). Cover the tin with two layers of carpet underlay or a similar material (1) holding it firm with elastic bands.

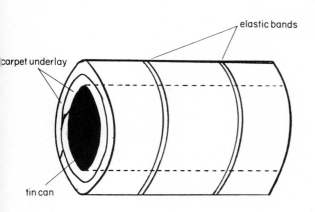

1 Constructing a cylindrical pillow: covering the core

Make a loose cover of strong, closely woven fabric, hemming each end to take a drawstring (2).

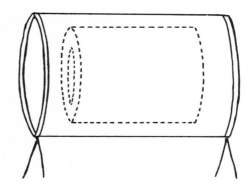

2 Adding a loose cover with hemmed edges and drawstrings

Fill the space between the cover and underlay with kapok (or a similar filling substance) – work from both ends and pack tightly. When the surface is smooth and firm, pull up the strings and fasten. Wedge the pillow into a shallow box (3).

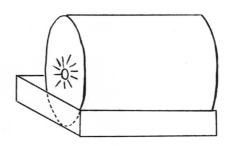

3 Wedging the pillow into a shallow box

From a sheet of foam approximately 25 cm × 45 cm × 1 cm (10 in × 18 in × ½ in) make an 'apron' to fit across the front of the pillow (4a). Cover the 'apron' with fabric, and attach elastic to hold it on the pillow (4b).

A more substantial cylindrical pillow involving some carpentry is described at the end of the book in the Appendix.

5 Constructing a flat pillow

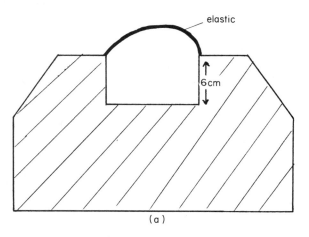

(a)

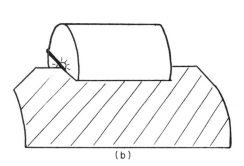

(b)

4 Adding an apron across the front

To make a flat pillow

Use a rigid board approximately 30 cm × 40 cm (12 in × 18 in). Make a bag of strong, closely woven fabric to just fit the wood. Pack stuffing – eg kapok or chopped straw – tightly and evenly on one side of the wood (5). Close the opening using a needle and strong thread.

Hammer the surface of the pillow and take up any slack this produces – by adding more stuffing, or pleating and sewing down the loose fabric.

Repeat the hammering and taking up slack process as often as necessary to make a smooth, firm pillow.

Bobbins

Up to twelve pairs of bobbins will be needed for the patterns in this book. Wooden bobbins like the one illustrated in **6** are very comfortable to use. These can be turned from dowelling on a small lathe. Other forms of bobbin are illustrated in **7**.

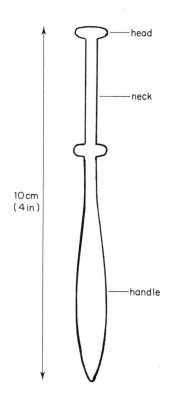

6 Turned wooden bobbin (actual size)

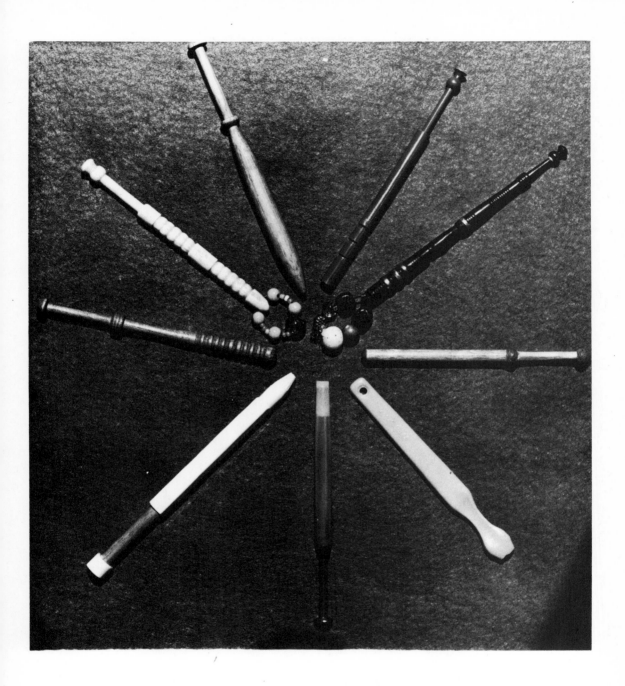

7 A selection of bobbins (clockwise from top right): (a) modern plastic bobbin; (b) antique wooden bobbin with pewter inlay and bead weights; (c) dowelling shaped with a penknife, plastic wood added for the head; (d) toothbrush handle warmed (over a candle) and stretched to give a neck; (e) three inch nail pushed into a fountain pen cartridge; (f) sections of felt-tipped pen for the handle and head with dowelling glued in position for the neck; (g) turned wooden bobbin; (h) antique bone bobbin with beads; (i) simple wooden bobbin

Patterns

Card is needed for the patterns – called 'prickings' – from which the braids are worked. Glazed card is most durable, but any strong card will do. Architect's tracing film may also be used (see chapter 4 and the Appendix).

Ruler and pencil, ball-point or marking pen

A ruler with a straight edge is required for marking out the first pricking.

Tracing paper and squared paper

Later prickings require the use of tracing paper. Squared paper is useful when designing prickings. Use 5 mm ($\frac{1}{4}$ in) squared paper for the Torchon patterns in chapter 7; a larger or smaller scale may be used if desired.

Pricker

This is for making the holes in the prickings. Make a pricker from a sewing needle held in a cork (**8a**), length of dowelling (**8b**) or a pin vice (**8c**).

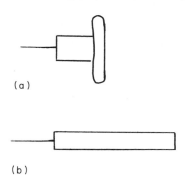

(a)

(b)

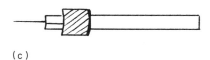

(c)

8 Prickers

Cork mat

A cork mat or stiff pad of fabric is required for laying the card on when pricking the pattern with a pricker.

Scissors

A large pair is required for cutting card and paper, and a short pair for trimming threads.

Sewing needles and crochet hooks

These are required for joining braids, making 'sewings', and adding beads. Choose the finest hook that will readily catch up the working thread.

Pins and pincushion

Pins hold the threads in position during work. Dressmaking pins may be used or, for fine work, brass lace pins. Keep the pins handy in a small pincushion.

Thread

For practice, use No 20 crochet cotton thread – this is available in numerous colours at most haberdashers – but experiment with all kinds and combinations of thread. No 10 and No 40 crochet cotton are also specified for some of the braids, as well as No 5 and No 8 cotton perle, and fine machine twist (normal sewing) thread. Double knitting and 4 ply wool make interesting braids (see chapter 3), and carpet thrums can also be used for some of the examples.

In the instructions for each item is a note of the materials used for the illustrated sample. This is intended as a guide to suitable threads and need not be followed rigidly.

2 Basic Techniques

The various techniques for making braids are identified in this and the following chapters by numbers preceded by 'T'.

9 Winding a bobbin

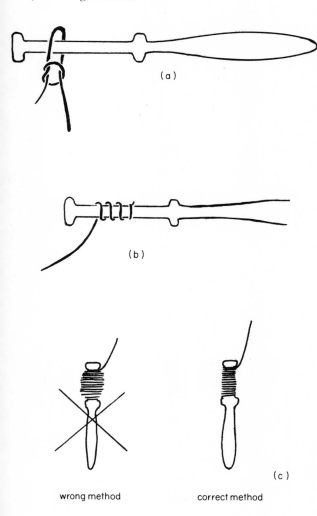

(a)

(b)

(c)

wrong method   correct method

T1: Winding bobbins

Tie an end of thread to the neck of the bobbin (**9a**). Turn the bobbin clockwise to wind on the thread (**9b**). Do not overfill the bobbin (**9c**).

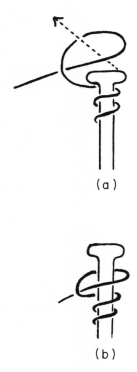

(a)

(b)

10 Securing the thread to prevent unwinding

Secure the thread with a slip knot (**10**). This prevents unwinding, while the working thread may be lengthened at will by turning the bobbin clockwise. To shorten the thread, release the knot and rewind.

T2: Four-strand plait

Wind four bobbins. Knot the four threads together. Pin the knot to the top of the pillow. Adjust the length of the working threads until all four bobbins lie on the foam 'apron' (11).

Take one pair of bobbins in each hand. *Twist* (tw) each pair by passing the right-hand bobbin over the left (12). Then *cross* (cr) the two inside threads, passing the left-hand bobbin over the right (13). Repeat these two movements to make a plait of the required length (14, 15). The movements of *twist* and *cross* are the basis of all the braids that follow.

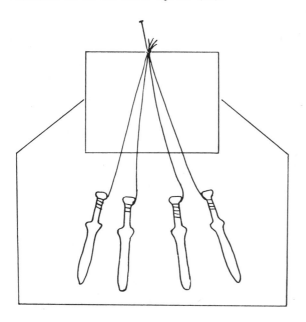

11 *Pillow and threads prepared for working a four strand plait*

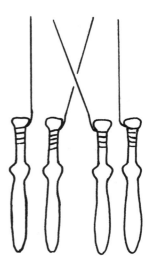

13 *Cross between two pairs*

12 *One pair twisted*

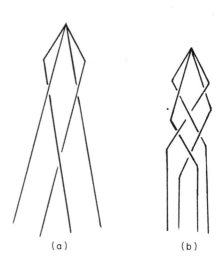

14 (a) *Two pairs twisted and crossed once;*
(b) *two pairs twisted and crossed twice*

15 *A four strand plait*

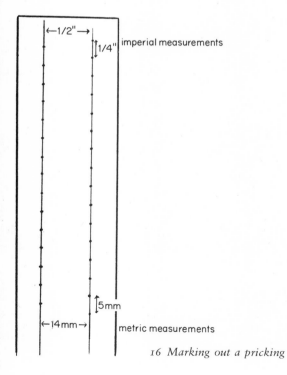

16 *Marking out a pricking*

imperial measurements

metric measurements

←1/2"→
↕1/4"
←14mm→
↕5mm

T3: Preparing a pricking

Use this method for braids approximately 1·4 cm (½ in) wide. Cut a piece of card about 2·5 cm (1 in) wide and long enough to go round the pillow. Use a pencil and ruler to mark the card (along its full length) as in **16**. Place the card on a cork mat or pad of fabric and use a pricker to make a small hole at each dot. Join the holes with an inked zigzag line.

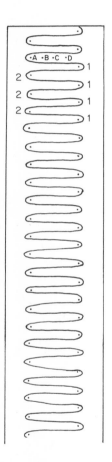

·A ·B ·C ·D

17 *The completed pricking*

Make three extra holes – B, C and D – these will only be used at the start of each braid. This completes the basic pricking (**17**), which is used for the braids at the end of this chapter and in chapter 3.

15

T4: Setting up the pillow

Wrap the pricking round the pillow matching the ends; fix with pins and, if necessary, a strong elastic band (18). Wedge the pillow in its box and put the apron in place.

18 Fixing a pricking to the pillow

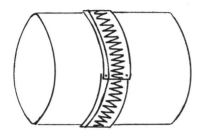

19 Seven pairs pinned to the pricking

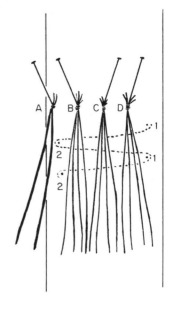

20 Cylindrical pillow set up with a pricking and seven pairs of bobbins

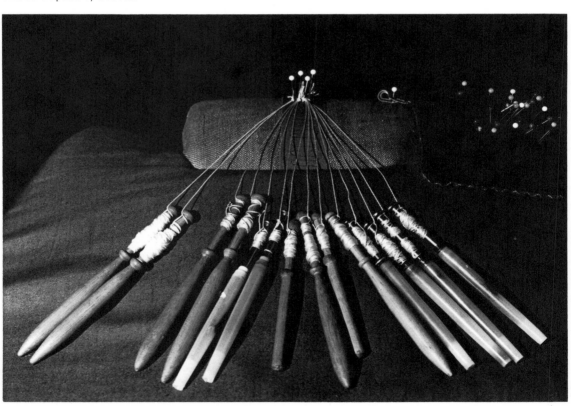

For the first samples, complete the following movements. Wind 14 bobbins: 12 in one colour, 2 in a contrast colour. Tie in pairs. Pin the contrast pair to the pricking at A. Pin 2 pairs at each of B, C and D (put pins through the knots, **19**). Adjust the threads to place the bobbins on the foam apron. Put spare pins beside the pillow.

Illustration **20** shows a pillow set up for the samples that follow.

T5: Whole stitch

The pair pinned at A are the 'workers' (wks), the others are 'passives'. Take the workers in the left hand and the first pair of passives (from B) in the right. *Cross/twist both pairs/cross. These three movements make a 'whole stitch' (w st) (**21a**). Push this pair of passives to the side and return the workers to the left hand. Pick up the next pair of passives with the right hand. Repeat from * (**21b**).

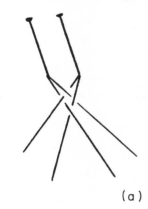

(a)

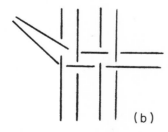

(b)

21 *Whole stitch: (a) one stitch worked;*
(b) two stitches

Work whole stitch with each pair of passives in turn (six altogether). Put in a pin at 1 between the workers and the last pair of passives (**22a**).

Work back across the braid making six more whole stitch – on this row the workers will be in the right hand at the start of each stitch. Put in a pin at 2 (**22b**).

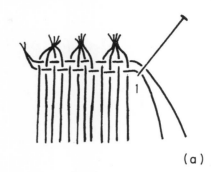

(a)

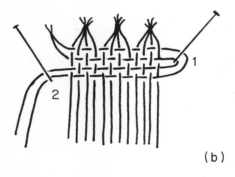

(b)

22 *(a) One row of whole stitch; (b) two rows*
of whole stitch

Remember that *cross* is *always* left over right between pairs; *twist* is right over left within a pair. Repeat from * until you make the stitch easily.

Samples of whole stitch, doubles and half stitch (T5, T6 and T7) may be worked as a continuous strip (as shown in **23**), or as three separate samples, setting up each as in T4.

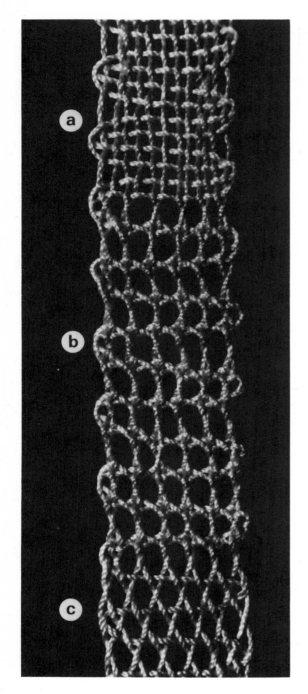

T6: Doubles

A 'double' (dbl) has four movements: twist (both pairs)/cross/twist (both pairs)/cross (**24**). Start on the left with workers in the left hand, passives in the right. Work a double with each pair of passives in turn, then put in a pin at 1 (**25a**).

 Continue working from side to side; **25b** shows the second row of doubles, with pin 2 in position. The passives may require a firm pull at the end of each row.

24 One double

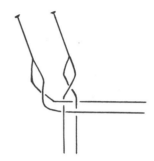

25 (a) One row of doubles; (b) two rows of doubles

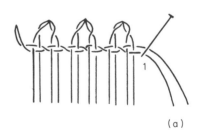

(a)

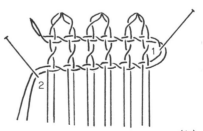

(b)

23 A sampler showing: (a) whole stitch, (b) doubles, (c) half stitch

T7: Half stitch

A 'half stitch' ($\frac{1}{2}$ st) has only two movements: twist (both pairs)/cross (**26**). As with whole stitch and doubles, two bobbins are laid aside after each stitch and a new pair picked up. However with half stitch the bobbins 'change partners' at each stitch, so pairs do not stay together as workers or passives. A sample of half stitch has one horizontal thread in each row with the other threads running diagonally (**27**).

26 One half stitch

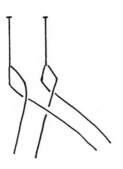

27 (a) One row of half stitch; (b) two rows of half stitch

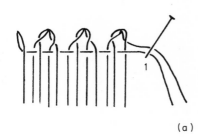

(a)

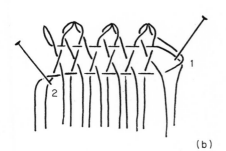

(b)

General points

(1) Rotate the pillow at intervals to keep the working area on top.

(2) Remove pins, carefully, when they are no longer necessary to hold the braid in shape.

(3) To finish a sample, simply cut the threads a few centimetres (an inch) from the work. For other ways of finishing see chapter 8.

(4) Most braids may be started as in T4, but for a neater start wind the bobbins in pairs as in T8.

T8: Winding bobbins in pairs

For each pair of bobbins: wind one bobbin as in T1; before cutting the thread, unwind an extra length of thread from the ball, wind this onto the second bobbin; leave a short length of thread between the bobbins, and hang this round a starting pin (**28**).

Work the first two or three rows of the braid, then remove the starting pins and pull gently on the bobbins to eliminate the loops of thread (**29**).

28 Two bobbins wound as a pair

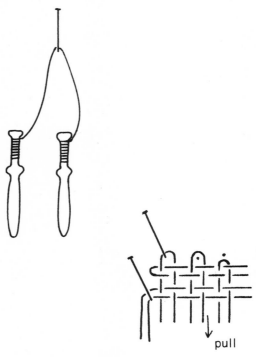

pull

29 Eliminating loops at the start of a braid

Replacing an empty bobbin

Wind a bobbin as in T1. Knot the end of the thread over one of the pins in the work. Secure the old thread under the hitch at the head of the bobbin (30). Work several stitches with this double thread. The ends of thread should be cut off close to the work when the pins have been removed.

30 Replacing an empty bobbin

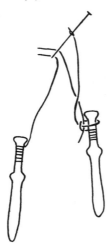

Notes on the use of a flat pillow

(1) Tilt the pillow towards you, eg by resting it against a thick book (31).

31 Tilting a flat pillow

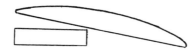

(2) For a straight braid make a pricking about three-quarters of the length of the pillow. Pin near the top of the pillow, along the centre (32).

(3) Cover the lower part of the pillow and pricking with a cloth on which to rest the bobbins (32).

(4) Start with the threads pinned at the top of the pricking.

(5) Have only a short thread, about 5–10 cm (2–4 in), between the bobbin and the worked braid.

(6) When the work reaches the foot of the pricking, pin the bobbins into the folded cover cloth

and support their weight while removing all the working pins, lifting the worked braid to the top of the pillow and repinning the last 8cm (3 in) to the top of the pricking (33).

32 Position of pricking and cover cloth on a flat pillow

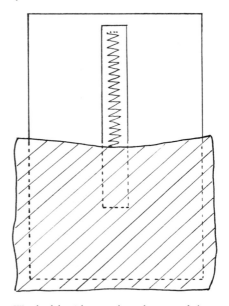

33 Worked braid moved to the top of the pillow with bobbins pinned into a cover cloth

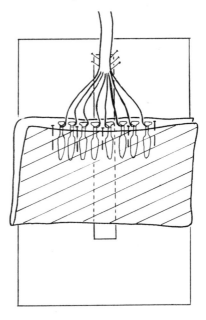

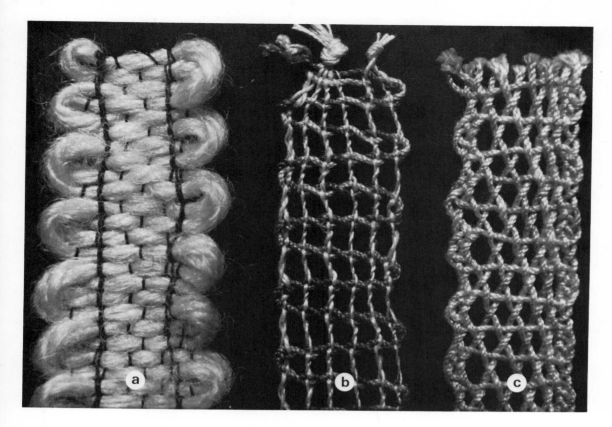

*34 (a) Whole stitch braid; (b) doubles braid;
(c) half stitch braid*

Simple braids

Braids may be worked in whole stitch or doubles
throughout, or various combinations of stitches
may be used. The pricking (**17**) prepared at the
start of this chapter is used for the three braids that
follow here, and for all those in chapter 3.

Whole stitch braid

Wind 1 pair with thick knitting yarn as workers
and hang at A. Wind 6 pairs with machine twist
and hang 2 pairs at each of B, C and D, as
passives. Starting from the left, work 6 whole
stitch on each row. The contrasting thicknesses of
thread cause the passives to become unevenly
spaced (**34a**).

Doubles braid

Hang 1 pair of No 20 crochet cotton at A
(workers). Hang 2 pairs of machine twist at
each of B, C and D (ie 6 pairs passives). Starting
from the left, work 6 doubles on each row (**34b**).

Half stitch braid

A half stitch braid usually needs the strength of
doubles on each edge, so for each row of this braid
(**34c**) work: 1 double; 4 half stitch; 1 double; put in
a pin. Use 7 pairs of No 20 crochet cotton, divided
between the starting pins.

For short, the above instructions can be written:
dbl/4 $\frac{1}{2}$ st/dbl/pin. This abbreviated form of
instructions is used throughout the book; see the
end of the book for a full list of abbreviations.

3   Basic Braid and its Variations

Use the pricking illustrated in **17** for all the braids in this chapter. The braid that is described here as the 'basic braid' consists of a central panel of passives worked in whole stitch, with an edge pair on each side worked in doubles (**35**).

35 One row of basic braid

The basic braid

First braid

For the basic braid in **36a**, wind 8 pairs with No 20 crochet cotton. Hang 2 pairs at each of A, B, C and D. Starting at A, and taking the left-hand pair as workers: * dbl/tw wks/5 w st/dbl/pin at 1 (**35**). Repeat from *; pin at 2. Repeat for the required length.

This basic braid has the two edge pairs and a central panel of 5 passive pairs. Braids **b** and **c** in **36** are also basic braids, made with 9 and 6 pairs of

36 Basic braids

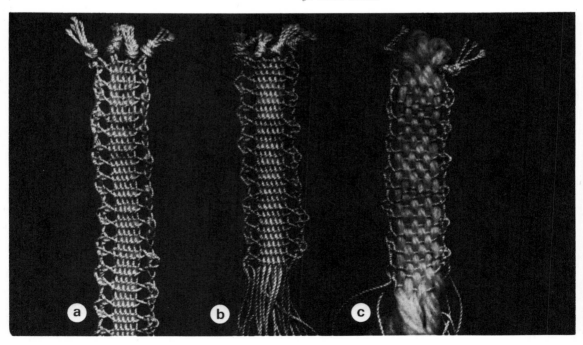

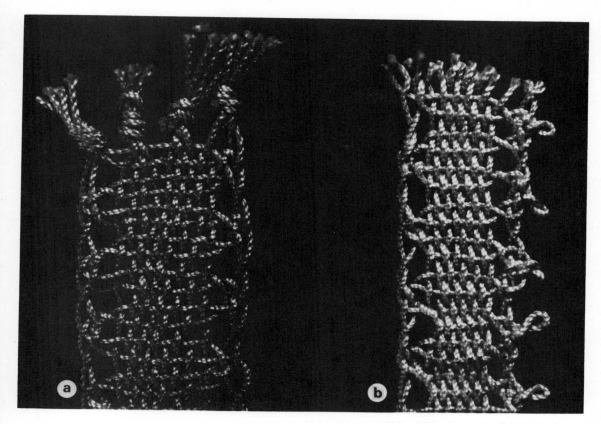

37 (a) Basic braid with closed edge; (b) basic braid with one closed and one picot edge

thread respectively. In **36b** the central panel is of 6 passive pairs, and 6 whole stitch are worked on each row, while in **36c** there are only 3 passive pairs and 3 whole stitch are needed.

Second braid

For **36b** use 9 pairs No 20 crochet cotton. Hang: 3 prs red at A; 2 prs red at D; 2 prs ecru at each of B and C. First row: dbl/tw wks/6 w st/dbl/pin.

Third braid

For **36c** use 3 pairs No 20 crochet cotton and 3 pairs Double Knitting wool. Hang: 2 prs red cotton at A, 1 pr at D; 2 prs yellow wool at B, 1 pr at C.

Braid variations

In addition to the variations produced by different colours and thicknesses of thread, the edge or the central panel of a basic braid may be modified in various ways (see T9 and T10, and T11 to T15 respectively).

Examples of T9 and T10 are shown in **37**. Both braids are worked with eight pairs – two pairs hung at each starting pin – and started on the left. The first row of the braid shown in **37a** is worked: dbl/* tw wks/5 w st/dbl †. The workers are then exchanged for the edge pair at the pin giving a straight, or 'closed' edge. To work a closed edge, see below.

The braid shown in **37b** has one closed and one 'picot' edge. Work as for **37a** until †, then make a picot, as described below.

23

T9: Closed edge

Put in a pin at 1 inside the last double (38). Take the threads nearest the pin as the workers for the next row and repeat from * to †; put in a pin at 2 beside the double. This gives a straight or 'closed' edge. Extra twists in both workers and edge pairs, before and after the pins, will give a firmer edge.

38 Forming a closed edge

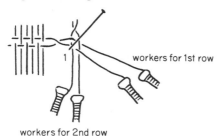

T10: Picot

Put in a pin at 1. Twist the pair nearest the pin (workers), take one thread round the pin (39a). Twist the pair twice more. Work a double with the edge pair (39b). Then continue the braid from * as for 37a.

39 Making a picot

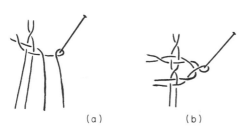

(a)   (b)

T11: Holes

A hole is made in the braid when either passives or workers are twisted. The braids in 40 (each worked with seven pairs) show some examples.

Basic braid with holes

The braid shown in 40a is worked as a basic braid except for the extra twists given to the workers between the central passives. The leaf-shaped hole is formed by making 1, 2, 3, 2, 1 twists on succeeding rows.

40 (a) Basic braid with holes; (b) ladder braid

Ladder braid

In 40b the ladder effect is the result of twisting the workers in the middle of each row and not at the edge. Each row is worked: dbl/2 w st/tw wks twice/3 w st/pin.

Thick threads

Thick threads may be introduced as workers (eg 34a) or passives (36c), or given greater emphasis in one of the following ways.

T12:Gimps

Inserting a gimp

Gimp threads are worked singly – all other threads are in pairs. To insert a gimp along the edge of a basic braid: hang on 8 pairs; knot the end of the gimp and pin to the right of the central passives (41a). * Work as for the basic braid until the gimp is reached, then pass the gimp between the workers (41b). Repeat from *. Twisting the workers before and after the gimp (41c) will give it further emphasis.

41 *Inserting a gimp*

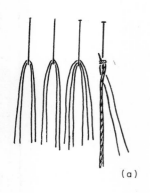
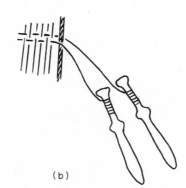
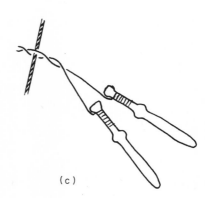

(a) (b) (c)

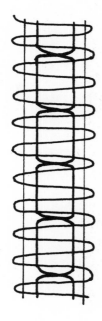

42 *Two gimps*

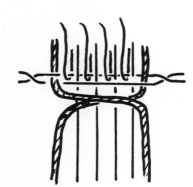

43 *Crossing two gimps*

Crossing two gimps

A possible arrangement of two gimps is sketched in 42. The gimps are placed on either side of the central passives and crossed after every fourth row. To cross the gimps: lift alternate passive threads, pass each gimp under these threads to the opposite side (43), then drop the passives into the correct positions.

T13:Cording

One or two pairs of thick threads are required. One pair gives the appearance of a raised cord (45a), two pairs that of a raised chain (45b).

Single cording

For 45a hang on 7 prs No 20 crochet cotton, and 1 pr 4 ply wool (in the middle of the passives) for cording. *Work to the centre as for the basic braid, twist the thick threads, then pass both workers between these threads (44). Finish the row as for the basic braid and repeat from *.

45 (a) Single cording; (b) chain cording

44 (a) Passing workers between threads for cording; (b) cording after two rows

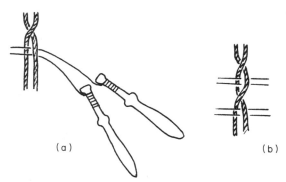

(a) (b)

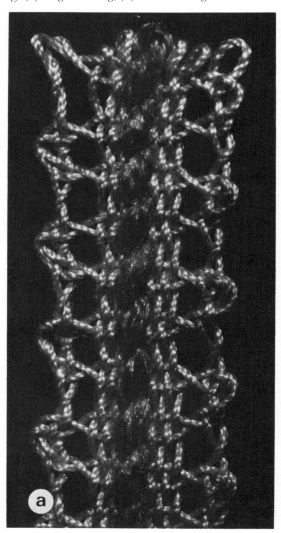

a

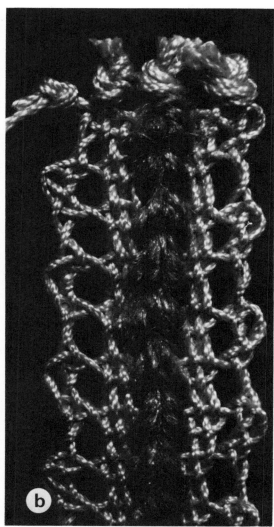

b

46 *(a) Passing workers between threads for chain; (b) second row of chain*

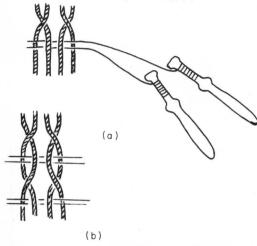

(a)

(b)

Chain cording

The cording in **45b** is worked in a similar way, but with two thick pairs in the centre of the passives. To get the chain effect one pair must be twisted the wrong way (ie left over right); this upsets the rhythm of work unless carried out as follows. *Work to the chain in basic braid; bring the two lower thick threads up between the others; pass both workers beneath the raised threads (**46**); repeat from *.

T14: Tallies

Small blocks, known as tallies, may be used to ornament braids. Tallies may be triangular, rectangular or leaf-shaped; four threads are needed for each tally. Practice will be needed to perfect these shapes.

47 *Working a tally*

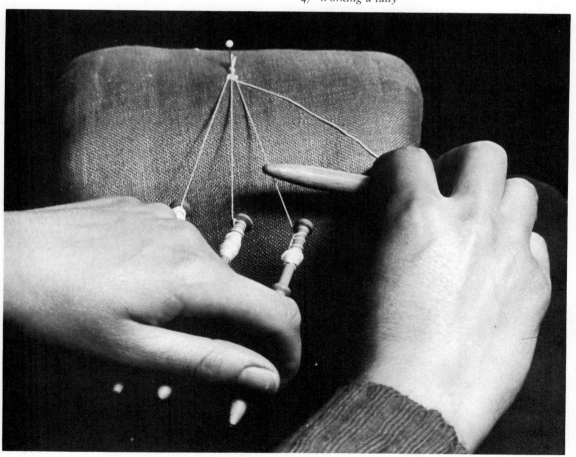

Leaf-shaped tally

Knot four threads together, pin through the knot. Hold three of the bobbins between the fingers of the left hand – **47** shows one way of doing this, or the hand can be held palm upwards if this is more comfortable. Use the right hand to weave the fourth bobbin, handle first, over and under the three threads. Control the shape of the leaf by the tension of the two outer threads – tight while the leaf is widening (**48a**), then relaxed slightly (**48b**).

48 *(a) Forming a leaf-shaped tally;*
(b) completed tally

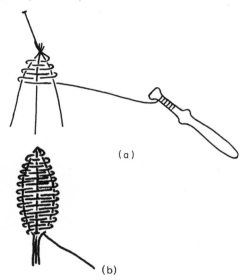

Rectangular tally

Knot 2 pairs of threads, pin a short distance apart (**49a**). Work as for the leaf, but keep the passive threads as near parallel as possible (**49b**).

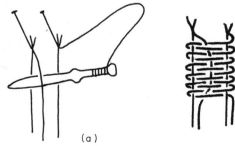

49 *(a) Forming a rectangular tally;*
(b) completed tally

Triangular tally

If the tally is started as a leaf and finished as for a rectangle (**50a**), or vice versa (**50b**), a triangle is formed.

50 Triangular tallies

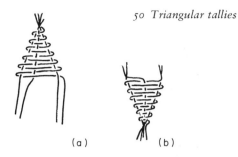

(a) (b)

Surface tallies

Basic braid with leaves
The braid shown in **52** is a basic braid with surface tallies. Hang on 12 pairs No 20 crochet cotton: 9 prs white; 3 prs gold – as 1st, 5th and 9th passive pairs. *Work two rows of basic braid. Throw back 4th and 5th passive pairs (**51**). Work two rows of basic braid without these two pairs. Bring forward the two pairs and work a leaf-shaped tally (about 10 weavings) using one of the gold threads as the weaver. Replace threads as central passives and repeat from *.

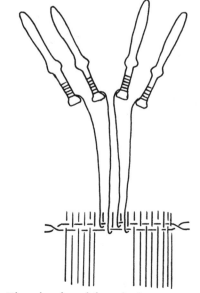

51 Threads selected for a leaf

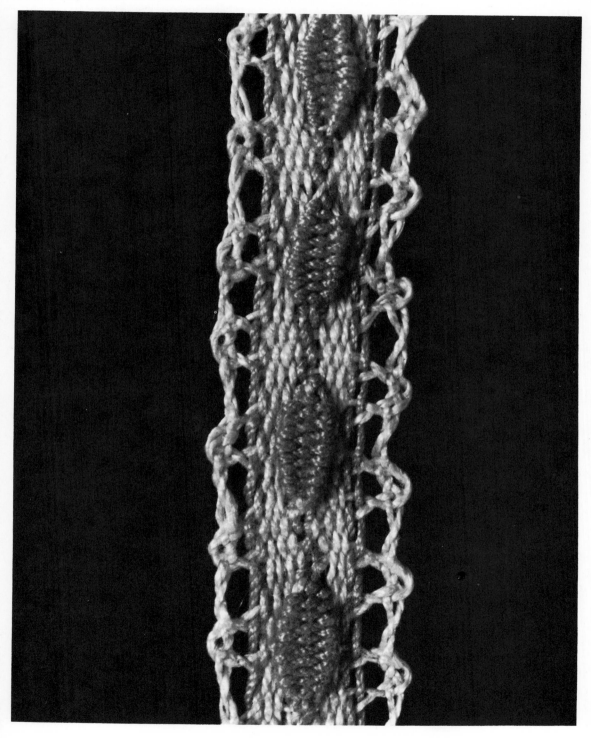

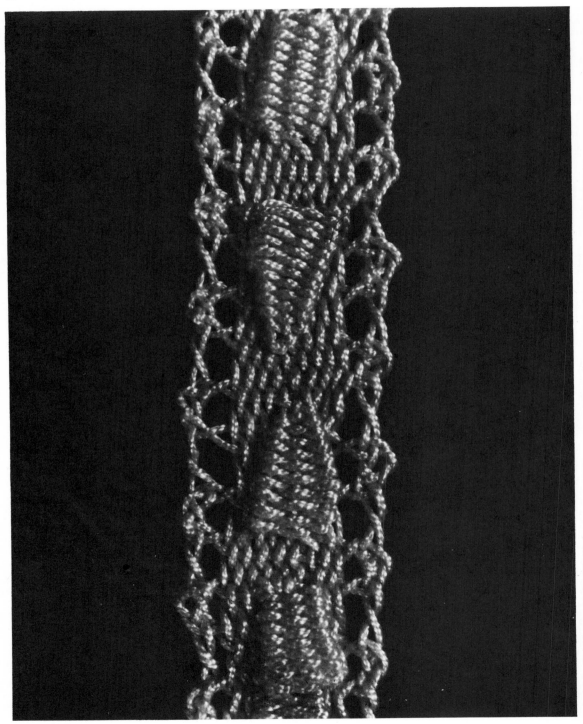

Sampler of tallies

The braid shown in 53 (worked with 11 pairs No 20 crochet cotton) has several different tallies. For the rectangle (top), throw back two pairs separated by two passive pairs (54). Work two rows of the basic braid, then bring forward the two pairs to work a tally of 12 weavings. Replace the threads.

54 Threads selected for a rectangle

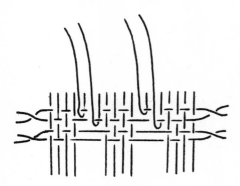

For the first triangle throw back 2nd and 7th passive pairs. Work the tally of 12 weavings over two rows of basic braid, then drop the threads into the central position. Reverse the procedure for the second triangle.

For the 'bobbles' at the foot of the sampler, work rectangular tallies of 12 weavings, using threads withdrawn on one row and replaced on the next. Place a matchstick, or similar, under the completed tally to retain its shape while working the next two rows (55).

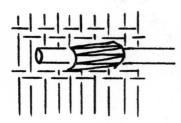

55 Forming a bobble

T15: Beads and sequins

There are several ways of working beads or sequins into a braid.

Threaded method

Arrange the beads as they will appear on the braid. String, in this order, onto the required threads before winding the bobbins – beads may be carried on workers or passives. While working the braid in the normal way push each bead to the top of the thread as it is needed leaving the other beads near the bobbin (56).

56 Beads on worker thread

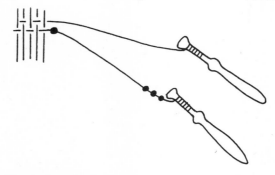

Hooked method

Work as usual to the point where a bead is wanted. Use a fine crochet hook to pull a loop of worker thread through the bead (57a). Pass the other bobbin of the pair through the loop (57b). Pull both threads tight.

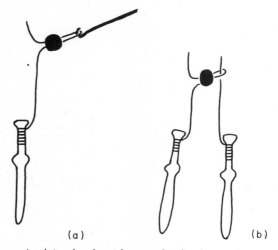

(a) (b)

57 Applying beads with a crochet hook

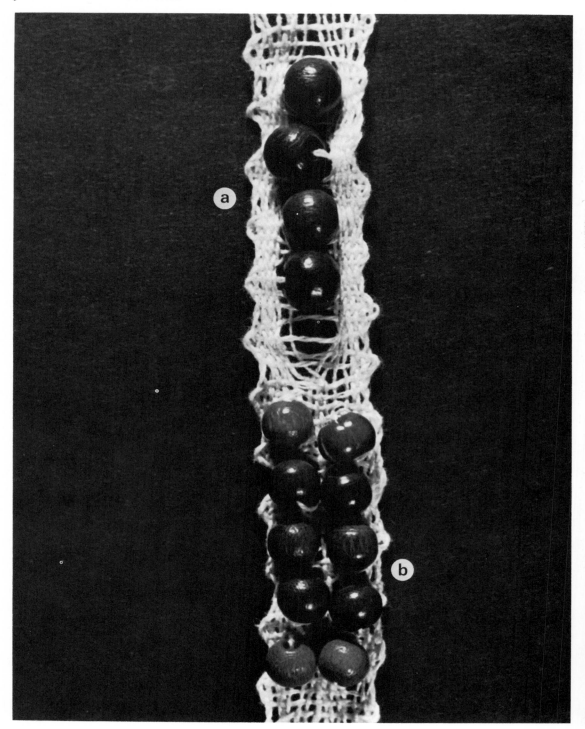

Arrangement of beads

Examples of beads worked into a whole stitch braid are shown in **58**. In part **a** the beads are carried on one of the workers, in **b** on two of the passives. In each case the beads are pushed into place on alternate rows.

Beads can also be carried on gimp threads, on the edge of a braid, for example, as sketched in **59**.

59 Beads on a gimp

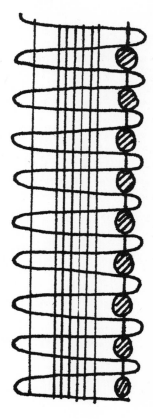

4 Straight Braids

Numerous braids can be worked on the first pricking (**17**), but other prickings will be needed for a greater range of designs.

T16: Making prickings
Each pricking is made on a piece of card 2 or 3 cm (1 in) wider than the braid and long enough to go round the pillow (if using a cylindrical pillow). Some prickings may be marked out by measuring – as was the first – but for many prickings tracing is easier.

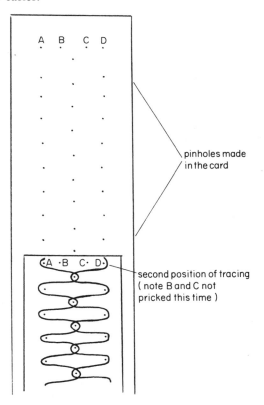

60 *Making a pricking from a tracing*

Trace the pattern taking particular care with the position of the pinholes. Fix the tracing to the card with adhesive tape. Prick the pinholes (see T3). Move the tracing along the card to repeat the pricking (**60**). Copy all markings onto the card.

For a pricking that will only be used once or twice, trace the pattern, with repeats if necessary, directly onto a piece of architect's tracing film. Pin the tracing to the pillow over a piece of plain paper. Pins will readily penetrate both film and paper so you can make the pinholes as you work. This method is particularly useful for copying a pattern with many loops and crossings, or when experimenting with a new pattern.

For most of the prickings only one worked example is given, but the use of different techniques, or threads of various colours and textures, will give individual results.

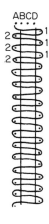

61 *Narrow pricking*

34

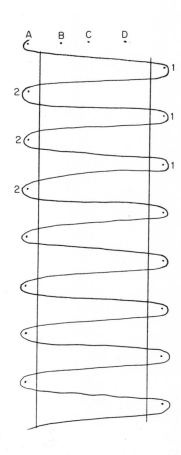

The prickings in **61** and **62** are simply smaller and larger scale versions of pricking **17**. Any of the braids in chapters 2 or 3 could be worked on these, one pricking being suitable for fine thread (eg machine twist) and one for string or wool.

Illustration **63** shows a whole stitch braid worked on pricking **62** with six pairs of handspun wool as passives, and one pair of 2 ply weaving wool as workers.

Lines on prickings are guides to the paths taken by pairs of threads. If every pair was shown the pattern could be confusing, so passives are often omitted or shown by a single line. The path of the worker pair(s) is always shown and that of any pairs used for an edging (as in prickings **65, 73, 75** etc).

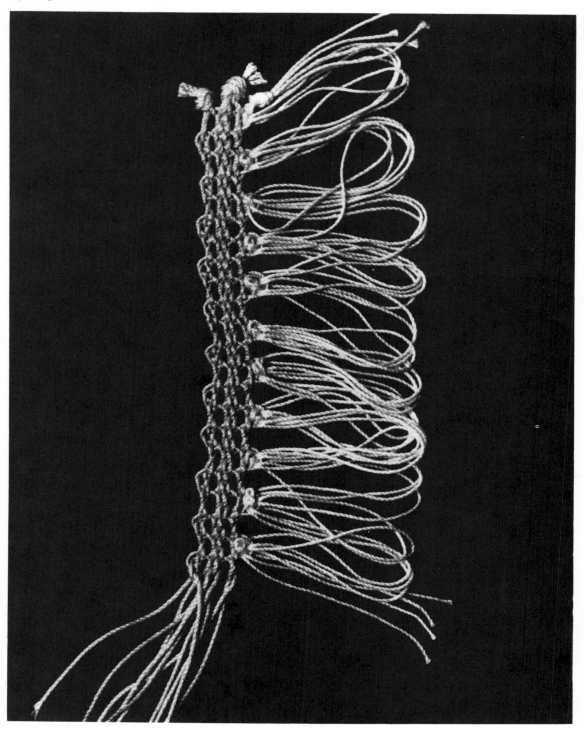

T17: Fringing

For the fringed braid illustrated in **64** use pricking **65** and six pairs of bobbins: 5 prs for a basic braid; 1 pr for the fringe – in the sample these bobbins are wound with double thread to give a thicker fringe.

65 Pricking for fringed braid

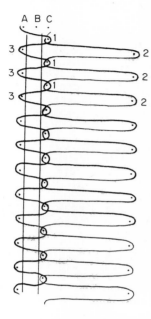

Hang 2 pairs at A, 3 pairs at B and the fringe pair at C. *Work as a normal basic braid to 1 (ie dbl/ tw wks/2 w st/dbl), then w st with workers and fringe pair/pin at 1/w st. Take the fringe pair round a pin at 2, and leave (**66**). Use the workers to continue with basic braid to 3. Repeat from *.

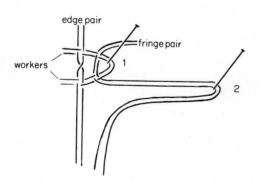

66 Forming a fringe

The position of the outer pins (2) controls the depth of the fringe. Shaped fringes may be produced like those in the sketch (**67**). The fringe may be cut or left as loops.

67 Shaped fringes

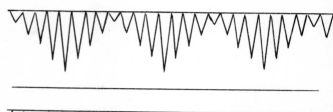

T18: Crossing three or four pairs

Braids may be edged with plaits or tallies. Where these join the main part of the braid three pairs of threads are involved. Four pairs are involved when two plaits (or tallies) cross.

(a) Crossing three pairs

Take the four bobbins from the plait (or tally) in one hand, the third pair in the other. Work a whole stitch with the four threads acting as a single pair (**68**).

(b) Crossing four pairs

This is the same principle as above, but with four bobbins held in each hand. A pin may be stuck in the centre of the stitch (**69**).

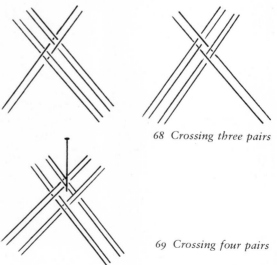

68 Crossing three pairs

69 Crossing four pairs

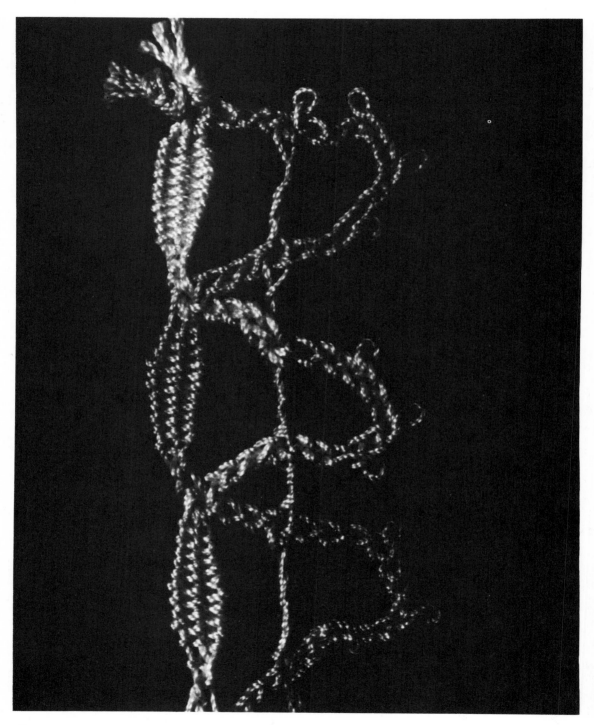

Plait and tally edging

The edging in 70 uses the above techniques to combine plaits and tallies. Prepare a pricking from 71 and five pairs of crochet cotton. Hang: 4 prs at A; 1 pr at B – this will be the only passive pair. *Work a tally with the two pairs from A (about 12 weavings) and leave.

With the other two pairs from A make a plait of two doubles, put both pairs in the left hand and work a whole stitch with the passives (ie 'cross 3 pairs'), then put in a pin at 1 through the stitch. Continue with the plait: (2 dbls/picot) 3 times/2 dbls; put pins for picots in 2, 3 and 4 (T10).

Then twist passives 4 times/'cross 3 pairs' with plait, pinning through stitch at 5. Plait a further 2 dbls/'cross 4 pairs' with the plait and tally/pin at 6. Twist passives 4 times. Repeat from * working the tally with the threads previously used for the plait and vice versa.

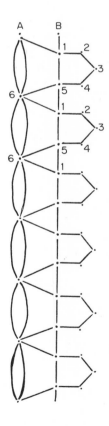

71 Pricking for plait and tally edging

Braid with a plaited edge

The braids in 72, 74 and 76 show a few of the possible arrangements of plaits and tallies on the edge of a braid.

For 72 use pricking 73 and eight pairs (No 20 crochet cotton). Hang: 2 prs at A; 3 prs at B; 1 pr at C; 2 prs at D– these will be for the plait. Starting at A: dbl */tw wks/3 w st/dbl/tw wks/'cross 3 prs' (with the 2 prs from D)/pin at 1/'cross 3 prs'/dbl/tw wks/3 w st/dbl/pin at 2 (on the right of dbl)/Work 4 dbls with the 2 pairs from D, take this plait round a pin at 3. Repeat from *.

72 Braid with a plaited edging

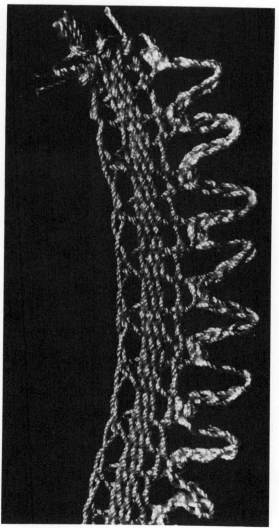

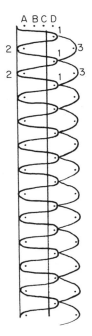

Braid with plait and picot edge

For **74** use pricking **75** and seven pairs. Hang: 2 prs at A, 3 prs at B, 2 prs at C – for the plait. Starting at A: dbl/* tw wks/3 w st/'cross 3 pairs' (with pairs from C)/pin at 1/'cross 3 pairs'. Continue with the main part of the braid: 3 w st/dbl/pin at 2 (beside dbl); tw wks/3 w st/pin at 3; 3 w st/dbl/pin at 4 (beside dbl). Make a plait with the threads from C: (dbl/picot) 4 times/dbl Repeat from *.

75 *Pricking for* 74

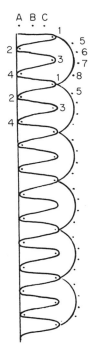

74 *Braid with plait and picot edge*

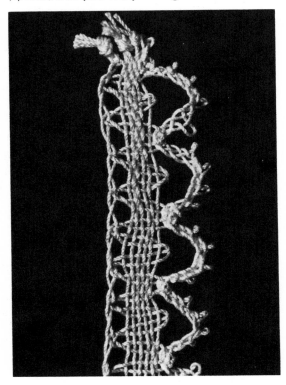

Edgings with plaits and tallies

Two plait edging

For the braid in **76a**, use pricking **77**, and nine pairs (No 40 crochet cotton). Hang: 2 prs at A, B and D; 3 prs at C. Use the 2 pairs from D and 2 of the pairs from C for the plaits, and the remaining 5 pairs to work a basic braid.

For the plaits work: 2 dbls between basic braid and first picot; 1 dbl between picots; 1 dbl between picot and crossing of 2 plaits. Where a plait meets the braid: 'cross 3 prs'/pin/'cross 3 prs' (T18a). Where 2 plaits touch: 'cross 4 prs'/pin/'cross 4 prs' (T18b).

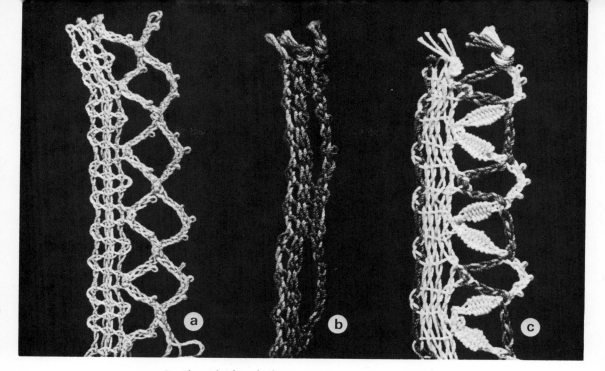

76 Braids with plaited edges

Whole stitch and plait edging

For the braid in **76b**, use pricking **78**, and six pairs (No 20 crochet cotton). Hang: 1 pr at A, 3 prs at B, 2 prs at C. Bring 1 of the pairs from B to the left: dbl with the pair from A. Work 2 rows in whole stitch with doubles on the left-hand edge. *Plait the 2 right-hand pairs: (2 dbls/picot) twice/2 dbls.

Use the other 4 pairs to work 4 rows of narrow braid: 1st row – dbl/tw wks/2 w st/tw wks †/pin; 2nd row – 2 w st/dbl/pin; 3rd row as 1st; 4th row as 2nd. Work the next row as the 1st as far as †, then: 2 w st with the threads of the plait/tw wks/pin at 10. Work three more rows with all the threads – starting with 2 w st/tw wks/2 w st – then repeat from *.

Braid with tally and plait edge

For the braid in **76c**, use pricking **79**, and ten pairs (No 20 crochet cotton): 6 prs for a half stitch braid; 4 prs (pinned at D) for the edging. Work the straight plaits with 2½ dbls. Put 1 dbl between picots. Make tallies of about 9 weavings. Work the half stitch braid with doubles on each edge (see **35c**). At 4 and 7: 'cross 3 prs'/pin/'cross 3 prs'. At 5 and 9: 'cross 4 prs' putting a pin through the centre of the stitch.

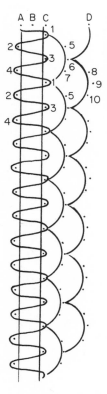

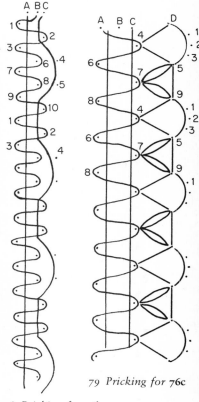

77 Pricking for **76a**

78 Pricking for **76b**

79 Pricking for **76c**

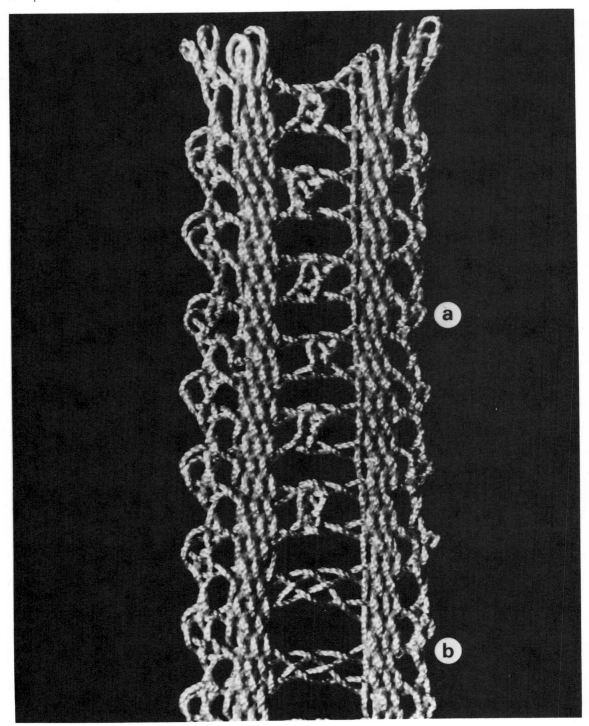

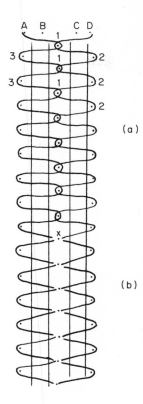

(a)

(b)

Linked Braids

Pricking **83** gives a very open braid, illustrated in **82**, with workers linked on alternate visits to the centre. Use eight pairs No 20 crochet cotton (4 prs red and 4 prs black). Each row of each half of the braid has 2 w st with a double beside the pin. Link the two pairs of workers as in **80a**. Braid **82** or **80** could be threaded with narrow ribbon.

82 (a) Linked braids

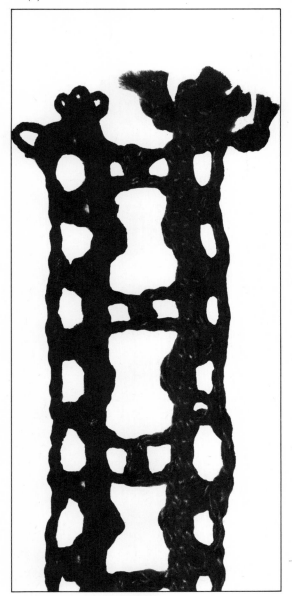

Open Braids

Many open braids have more than one pair of workers. The braid in **80** shows two ways of using two pairs of workers. Use pricking **81** and ten pairs. For each half of the braid hang on: 1 pr workers; 1 edge pr and 3 prs passives.

For part **a**, *starting on the left: dbl/tw wks/3 w st/leave. Starting on the right: dbl/tw wks/3 w st/leave. With the 2 pairs of workers: dbl/pin at 1/dbl. Take each pair of workers to its original side working: tw wks/3 w st/dbl/pin. Repeat from *.

For part **b**, work as **a**, except where the workers meet work: $\frac{1}{2}$ st/pin at $x/\frac{1}{2}$ st. This will take the workers to the opposite sides for the next row.

The effect of both parts is of two half basic braids linked together. Any of the variations in chapter 3 may be substituted for the basic braid on one side or both.

Braids with two passive pairs

All the braids illustrated in **84** and **86** have two or more pairs of workers. Pricking **85** is used for both the braids in **84**.

Braid with picots

For the braid in **84a**, hang on five pairs: 1 pr passives plus 1 pr workers at A; 2 prs workers at B; 1 pr passives at C. The path of each pair is shown on part **a** of the pricking. Work: doubles wherever two pairs cross; closed edge (T9) at pin 1; picot (T10) at pin 2.

Straight-sided braid

For the braid in **84b**, use six pairs – hang the extra pair of workers at C. Work as **84b**, but working a closed edge on the right instead of picots. Part **b** of the pricking shows the path of each pair.

82 (b) Detail of links

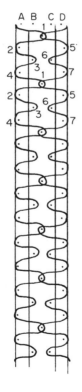

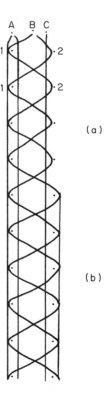

83 Pricking for 82

85 Pricking for 84

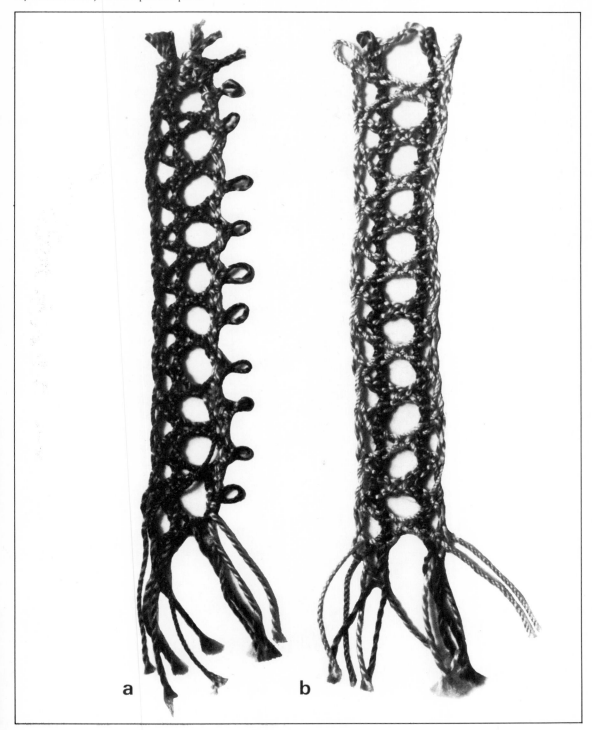

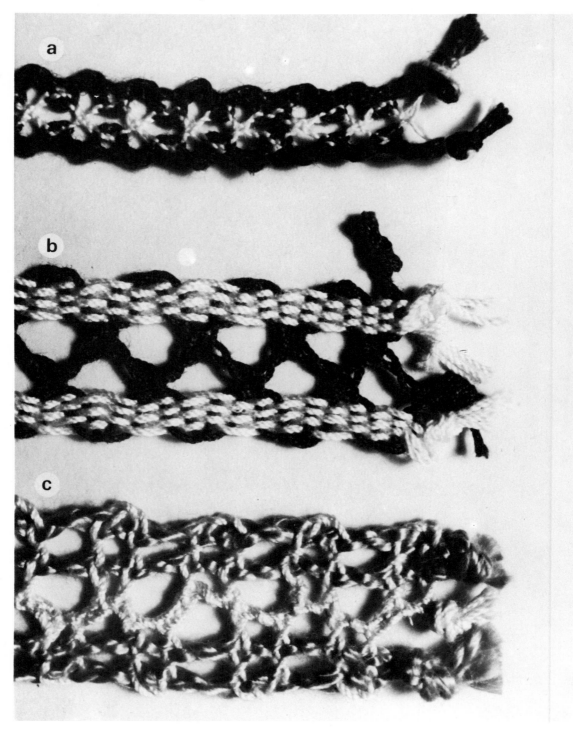

Braids with two or more worker pairs

Narrow braid

For the braid in **86a**, use pricking **87**. Worked in machine twist thread, this makes a dainty trimming for baby clothes. Use six pairs: 2 prs passives – 1 on each edge; 4 prs workers. Work this braid entirely in doubles: one in the centre (where there is no pin), and one before and one after each pin.

Braid with three worker pairs

For the braid in **86b**, use pricking **88**, and nine pairs: 3 prs workers (red in sample); 6 prs passives (white). Hang on: 4 prs at A (3 prs passives, 1 pr workers), 2 prs at B (workers), 3 prs at C (passives).

The paths of the three pairs of workers are indicated on the pricking. Start with the two pairs from B: dbl/take one pair to the right, tw/3 w st with passives from C. Tw wks again at the pin. Next work 3 w st with workers and passives from A. Proceed, following the pricking, working doubles where 2 pairs of workers cross – at *a*, *b* etc – and whole stitch with the passives.

Braid worked in doubles

For the braid in **86c**, use pricking **89**, and six pairs. Hang: 2 prs workers at B; 2 prs passives at each of A and C. Start from B taking one pair to the left. Work entirely in doubles. In the centre of the braid work two doubles with the two pairs of workers.

87 *Pricking for* **86a**

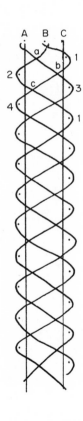

88 *Pricking for* **86b**

89 *Pricking for* **86c**

47

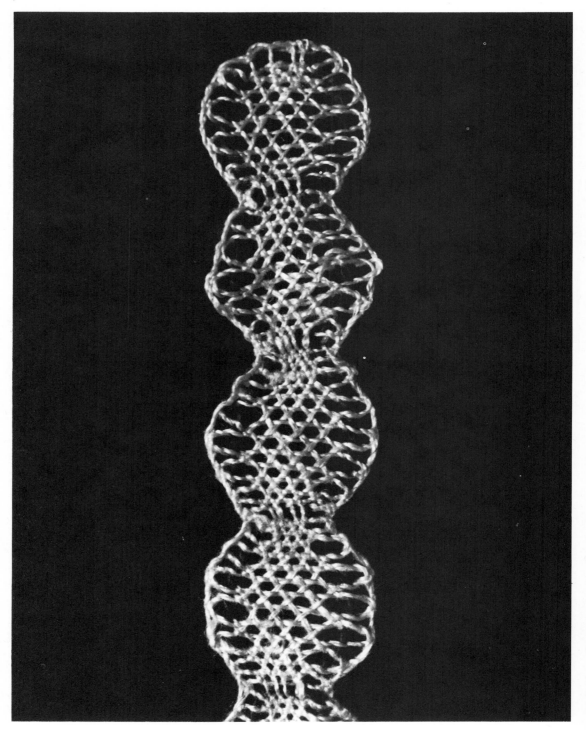

Torchon bookmark worked in cotton perle
(see fig 195)

Bookmark in half stitch, made with lurex and cotton perle
(see fig 196)

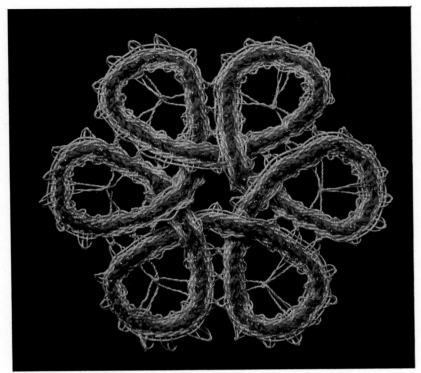

Flower motif with six petals worked in crochet cotton, perle glitter and machine twist (see fig 179)

Evening purse with lace motif in white cotton perle and lurex with glass beads (see fig 204)

Oval braid

Illustration **90** shows the effect of working a half stitch braid on pricking **91**. Hang seven pairs machine twist at A, with one pair of thicker thread for the gimps. Position the gimps between 1st and 2nd, and 6th and 7th pairs. Work in half stitch with closed edge – start with 2nd and 3rd pairs from the left. Twist workers before and after the gimps (**41c**). Cross the gimps before inserting the pin at 12 (**43**).

91 Pricking for 90

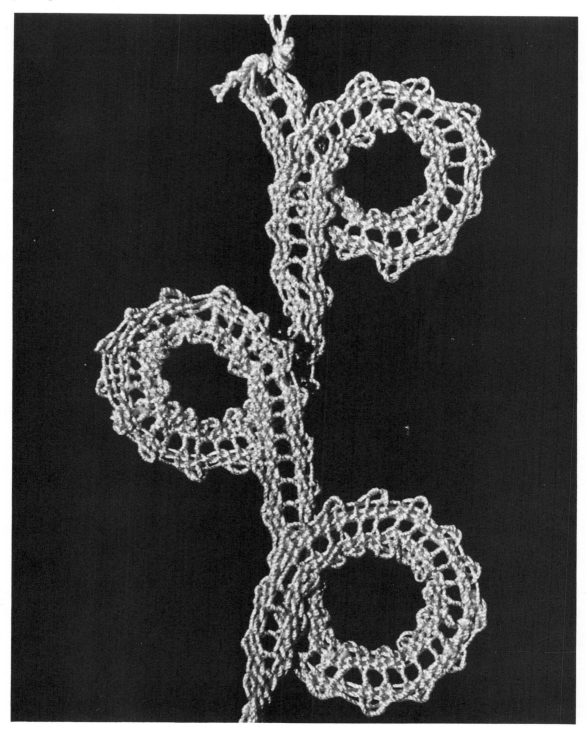

5 Curves and Angles

Rings of braid

A braid may be curved simply by reducing the space between the pinholes on one edge. The rings in **92** (pricking **93**) were made in this way. A 'ladder' braid (see **41b**) is shown in this sample, but any simple braid could be used on this pricking or the others in this chapter.

Hang on five pairs and work the braid in the normal way. As the ring is formed it will be necessary to turn the pillow, and to push the earlier pins well down so they do not catch on the threads. Before working pin 25, remove pins 2 to 7. Stick pins 25 to 32 through the worked braid.

Loops of braid worked close together may be linked with 'sewings'.

T19: To make a 'sewing'

Bring the workers to the point X to be linked; twist twice. Remove the pin from X. With a crochet hook bring one worker thread through X (**94a**). Pass the other bobbin, tail first, through the loop of thread thus formed (**94b**). Pull both threads tight. Twist and continue with the braid (**94c**). (The number of twists before and after a 'sewing' may be varied.) Three examples of looped braids linked by 'sewings' are shown in **95**.

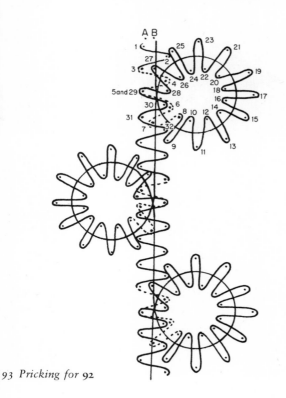

93 Pricking for 92

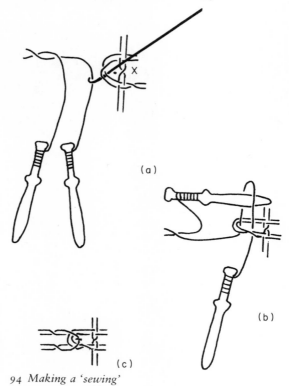

94 Making a 'sewing'

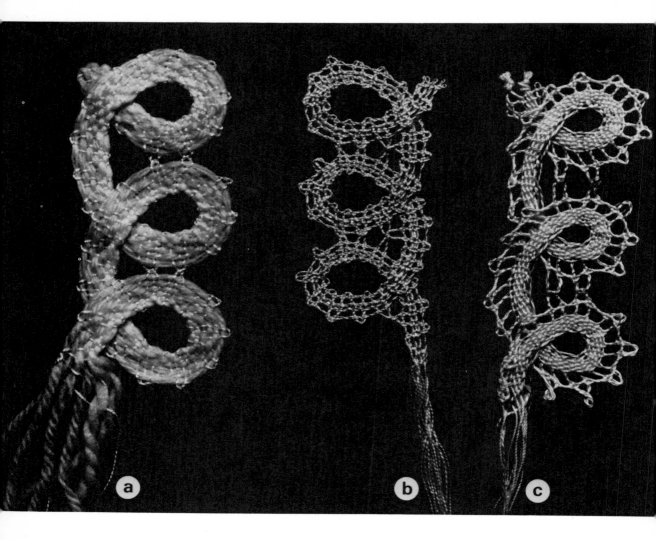

Looped braids with 'sewings'

Looped whole stitch braid

For the braid shown in **95a**, use pricking **96**, and 4 pairs: 3 prs DK wool as passives; 1 pr No 20 crochet cotton as workers. Work a braid in whole stitch until pin 14 of the second loop is in place. Remove pin 8 of the first loop and make a 'sewing'. Continue with the braid making a second 'sewing' at 6.

Looped basic braid

For the braid shown in **95b**, use pricking **97**, 6 pairs: 1 pr lurex thread as central passives; 5 prs

No 8 cotton perle as workers and other passives. (Note that this sample has been photographed from the back.)

Work in basic braid with normal 'sewings' at 10 and 8. The 'sewing' at 6 is slightly different since the workers come to the pin three times. For the first and second times, give five or six twists to the workers and take them round the pin, on the third time give three twists, then make a 'sewing' with the crochet hook going through both loops (**98**), and twist three times.

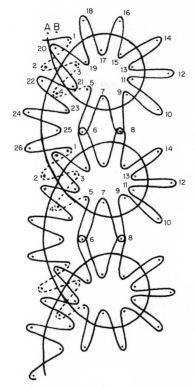

96 *Pricking for* 95a *and* 95c

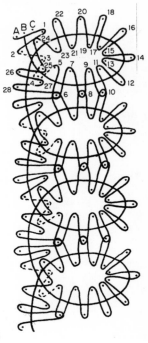

97 *Pricking for* 95b

Looped braid with turning stitch

The braid in **95c** is worked on pricking **96**, using just even-numbered holes with turning stitches on the other edge (see below for turning stitch). Hang on 6 pairs: 4 prs No 20 crochet cotton (white) at A and B – passives; 2 prs No 8 cotton perle (gold) at 1 – workers. *Take the second pair from the right as workers and work towards the left. First row: 3 w st/dbl/pin. Second row: dbl/tw wks/4 w st (the last w st is the turning stitch). Repeat from *. Make sewings at 6 and 8.

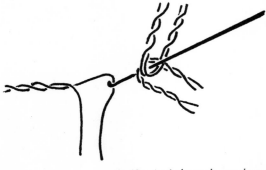

98 *'Sewing' through two loops*

T20: Turning stitch

Pins may be omitted on the inside of a curve, particularly where the curve is a tight one. Where there is no pin the last stitch worked in the row is a 'turning stitch'. After this stitch the workers are left while the other pair become the workers for the next two rows (**99**). The turning stitch can be a whole stitch, double or whole stitch plus a half stitch.

99 *Whole stitch used as a turning stitch*

Wherever a pricking is marked ⊃ without a pinhole, a turning stitch is worked.

53

Waved braids

The waved braids in 100 have turning stitches on both sides. In each of the three braids the edge pair is left unworked for one or more rows while the turning stitch is made with the pair before it.

'Hairpin' waved braid

For the braid in 100a, use pricking 101, and 5 pairs: 2 edge pairs (red cotton perle No 8), 1 hung at A, 1 at C; 3 pairs (white crochet cotton No 20) hung at B to alternate as passives and workers. Work entirely in doubles. Make turning stitches – with white pairs – between pins 6 and 7, 9 and 10 etc. Make 'sewings' at 5, 3 and 1, and 12, 11 and 10.

100 *Waved braids*

Serpentine braid

For the braid in 100b, use pricking 102, and 8 pairs No 20 crochet cotton: 1 pr at A; 2 prs at C; 5 prs – including a contrast pair – at B. With the two pairs from C: dbl/pin at 1/dbl/tw both pairs. Leave the right-hand (edge) pair on one side until just before pin 7. Take the other pair as workers: 5 w st/dbl/pin (at 2); *dbl/tw wks/5 w st/turn; 4 w st/dbl/pin. Repeat from * until pin is stuck at 6, then: dbl/tw wks/5 w st/dbl (with pair from 1)/pin at 7.

Work two more rows across all pairs, then leave the left-hand edge pair unworked until just before pin 14. Make 'sewings' at 6 and 13.

The sample and pricking show how the braid may be taken round a corner. A similar corner could be designed for 100c.

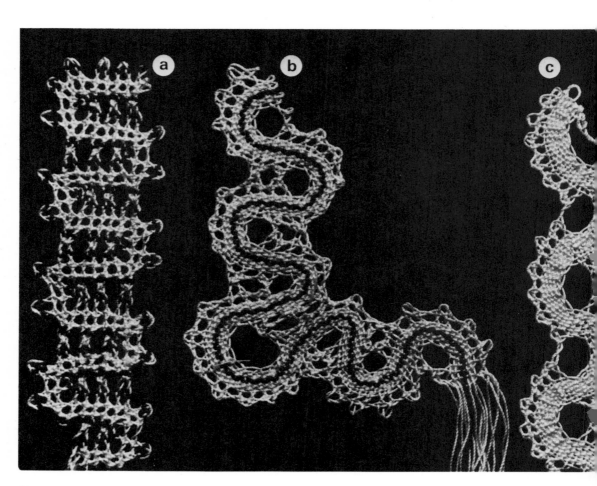

Lightly waved braid

For the braid in 100c, use pricking 103, and 8 pairs No 20 crochet cotton. Hang: 1 pr at A; 5 prs at B; 2 prs at C. There are no 'sewings', but otherwise the method of working is similar to that of 100b.

101 Pricking for 100a

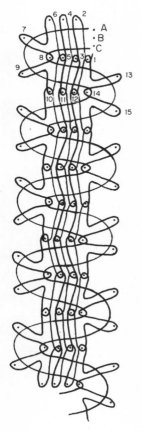

102 Pricking for 100b

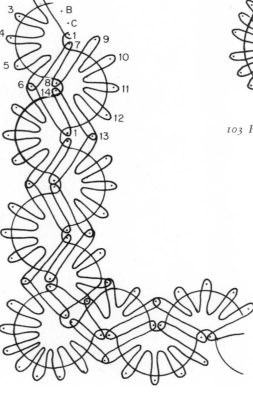

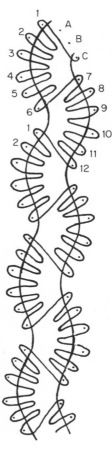

103 Pricking for 100c

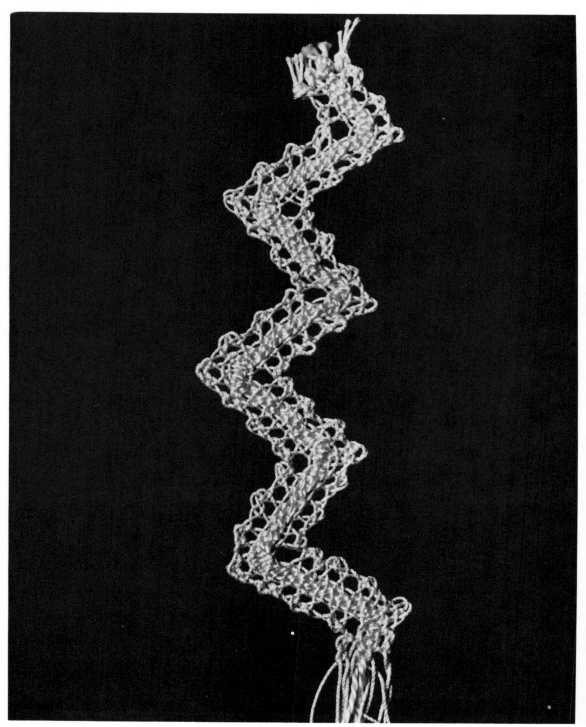

Angled braid

Turning stitches may also be used to produce sharp angles as in 104. Use pricking 105, and 6 pairs No 20 crochet cotton. Work in basic braid. After pin 2, leave the inside pair unworked, and make one turning stitch before and one after pin 4.

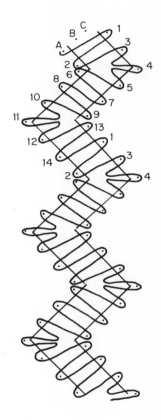

105 Pricking for 104

Further examples of the use of 'sewings' and turning stitches are given in chapters 8 and 9.

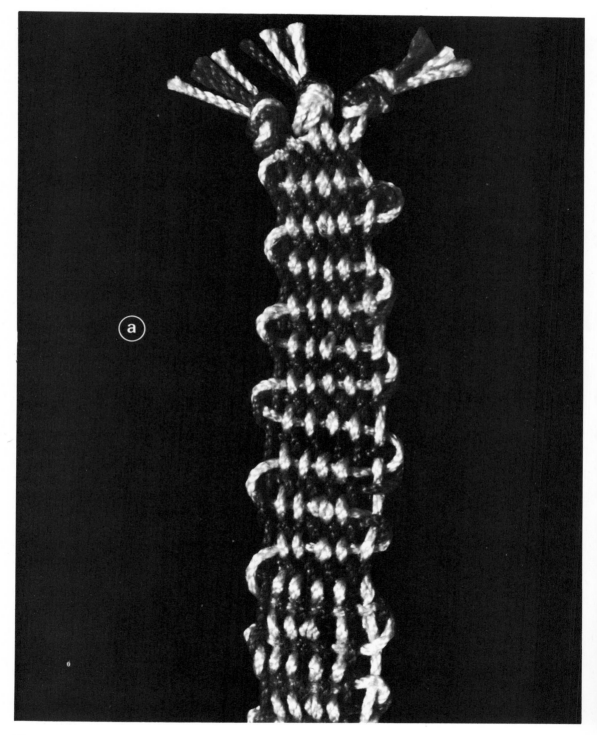

6 Patterned Braids and Edgings

This chapter contains designs for braids which include new ways to work the earlier prickings as well as many new prickings.

Striped braid

Braid 106 (pricking 107) is worked in whole stitch with 6 pairs, each pair consisting of one white and one red thread. In part **a** the white worker passes over the red passives and the red worker over white passives. In **b** the white worker goes under the red passives and vice versa. In each case the workers are twisted once at the pins. Slight rearrangements of threads, extra twists, etc, will give different effects, as in **c**.

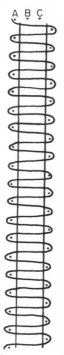

107 Pricking for 106

106 Striped braid

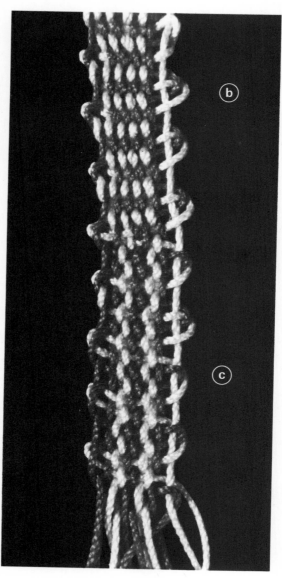

Spotted braids

The braids in **108** and **109** (worked on pricking **17**) show how cording and chain may be used to give spots of colour. Eleven pairs of thread are required including two contrast threads: pair each contrast thread with one of the main colour.

For **108** the contrasts should be the 10th and 15th threads from the left. Work a basic braid with two lines of cording (T13a)— one after the second and one after the fourth whole stitch of each row.

For **109** the contrasts should be in the centre of the braid and lifted together on alternate rows as a chain (T13b) is worked.

108 Spots produced by cording

109 Spots produced by chain

Braids with surface contrasts

With the braids in 110 (also worked on 17) the contrast threads do not form part of the braid, but are carried across the surface and attached by passing under, or between, the workers at appropriate points.

Illustration 110a shows a basic braid worked with six pairs No 20 crochet cotton. On the surface is a plait made with two pairs of a slightly thicker thread. The plait is linked to the braid on every third row by 'crossing 3 pairs' (T18a) beside the central passives. Each piece of plait is three doubles.

For 110b a braid as in 40b is worked, while a strand of wool is taken from side to side of each half, going under the workers at the centre of every fourth row and at alternate pins on each edge.

110 Surface contrasts

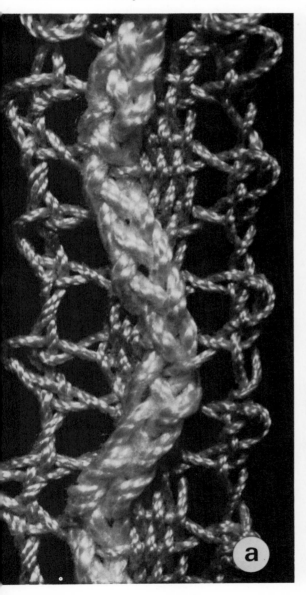

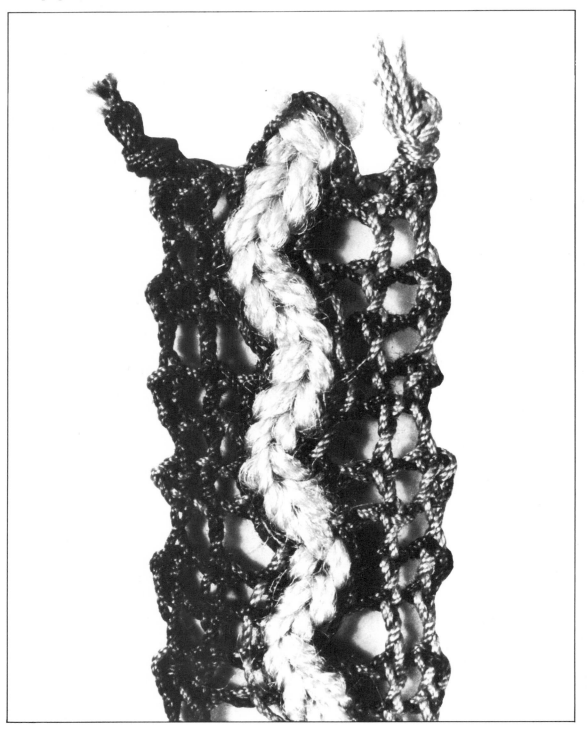

Zigzag chain

In 111, pricking 112, the zigzag is worked as a chain (T13b) and is an integral part of the braid. Use 7 pairs No 20 crochet cotton and 2 pairs 4 ply wool. Hang the 2 pairs of wool at B with a pair of cotton on each side. Hang 3 pairs at A and 2 pairs at C.

Take the third pair from the left as workers and go to the right: w st */chain/w st/2 dbls/pin (at 1); second row: 2 dbls/tw workers/w st/chain/w st/2 dbls/pin (at 2); third row: 2 dbls/tw workers/w st/chain/w st (this is a turning stitch). Take the passives as the new workers and repeat from * going first towards the left.

112 Pricking for 111

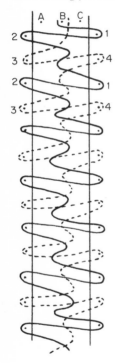

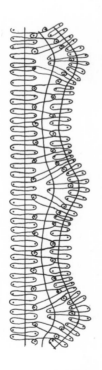

114 Pricking for three linked braids

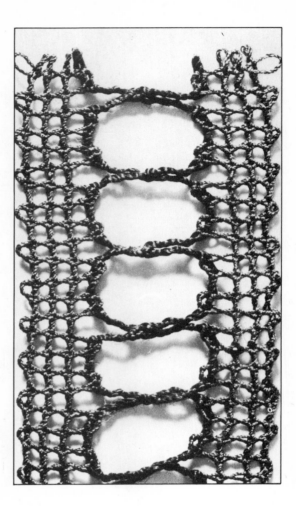

113 Linked braids

Linked braids

In 113 two braids are spaced and linked by two pairs of thread which are taken from side to side. Both pairs are twisted four times before and after a double in the centre. The rest of the sample is all doubles, but other braids could obviously be linked in this way.

The pricking in 114 can be used with machine twist (or other fine thread) for working three linked braids: for example, two whole stitch braids in a dark shade, linked by a lighter braid worked in doubles. Three or four pairs will be ample for each braid. The zigzag lines show the paths of the workers. Work: dbl/pin/dbl where two pairs meet.

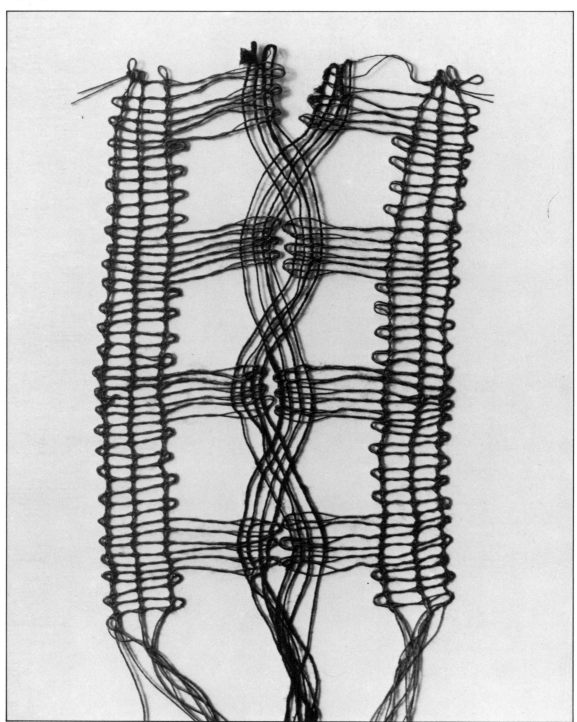

116 Pricking for 115

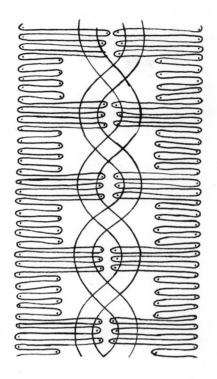

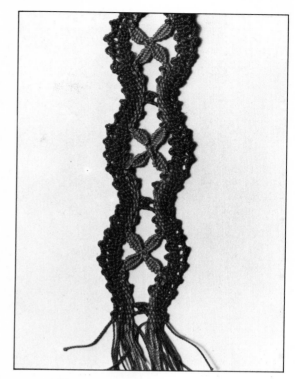

117 Oval braid with tallies

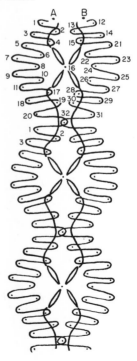

Fragile braid

The example shown in **115** is a rather fragile braid, and not one to withstand heavy handling. It could look very effective on a lampshade, for example. Use twelve pairs (8 of one colour, 4 in a contrast colour), and pricking **116**. Work the three passive pairs on each side in doubles, the central contrasts in whole stitch. Twist the workers four times between the two parts. Slightly rough threads – in the sample ropemaker's thrums – help retain the shape of the stitches.

Oval braid with tallies

The braid in **117**, pricking **118**, is also worked with twelve pairs (8 red, 4 orange No 20 crochet cotton). Each side of the braid is whole stitch with doubles on the outer edge. Tallies are of six weavings with a 'cross 4 prs' at 16. After pins 4 and 15, and before 17 and 28, 'cross 3 prs' treating the two pairs of the tally as one. At 32, dbl/pin/dbl with the two pairs of workers.

118 Pricking for 117

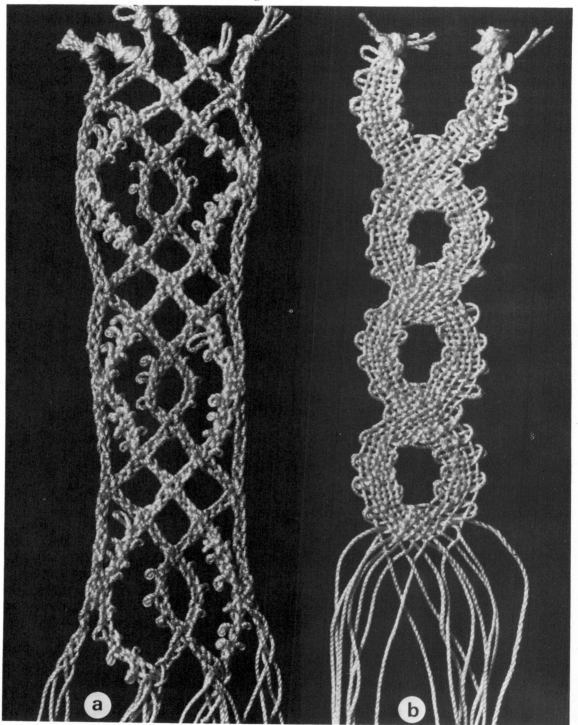

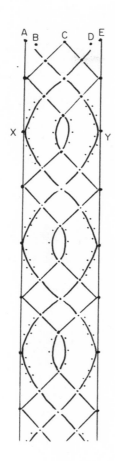

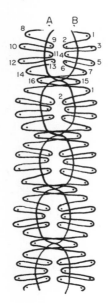

Braid with whole stitch rings

Each half ring of **119b**, pricking **121**, is a whole stitch braid worked with four pairs (3 prs passives, 1 pr workers). After pins 7 and 14, bring both pairs of workers to the centre, and work a whole stitch before taking them to the opposite side and round pins at 15 and 16. Still using whole stitch, take each right-hand passive pair in turn to the left. Then return the two worker pairs to their original sides (**122**).

Plait and picot braid

The braid in **119a** is based on a pattern that appears in one of the earliest lace books: *Le Pompe*, printed in 1559. Use pricking **120** and 12 pairs No 20 crochet cotton: 4 prs white – 2 prs hung at each of B and D; 8 prs orange – 2 prs at A and E, 4 prs at C. The lines on the pricking show the course of six separate plaits. Where two plaits cross, 'cross 4 pairs'. At X and Y use one white pair to 'cross 3 pairs'/pin/'cross 3 pairs' with the edge plait. Work four doubles between pins for the long plaits on the edge, two doubles for the short plaits, one double where there are picots on one side of the plait and a half stitch where there are picots on both sides.

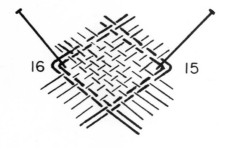

122 *Crossing threads for* 119b

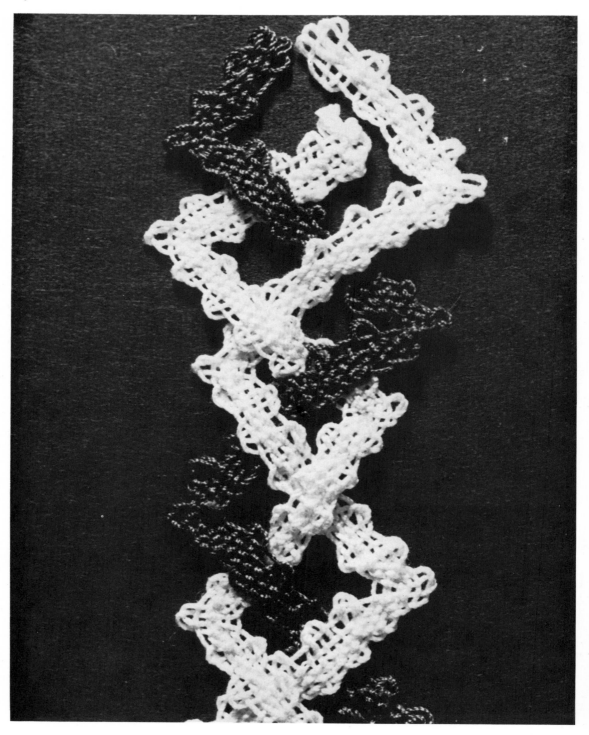

Plaited angled braids

Illustration **123** shows three whole stitch braids – with angles as in **104** – worked separately, then intertwined as though working a three-strand plait.

Trefoil worked in tenstick

Illustration **124** shows braid which does not require a pricking. It is the simple braid often known as 'tenstick' (from the ten bobbins usually used) that forms stems, outlines, flower centres, etc, in Honiton lace. It is easily worked even along quite tight curves. A line drawn on paper or tracing film is needed to indicate the course of the braid. Pin five pairs at the start of the line to work a braid that has a closed edge (T9) on the outside of any curve and turning stitches on the inside with two whole stitches between (**125**). Place pins for

124 Trefoil worked in 'tenstick'

125 Two rows of 'tenstick'

the outer edge at suitable points along the line. Usually two or three twists are given to both pairs on the outside edge, and the turning stitch is a whole stitch plus a half stitch – ie cr/tw/cr/tw/cr.

Four or six pairs may be used instead of the usual five. The trefoil illustrated was worked face down on the pillow.

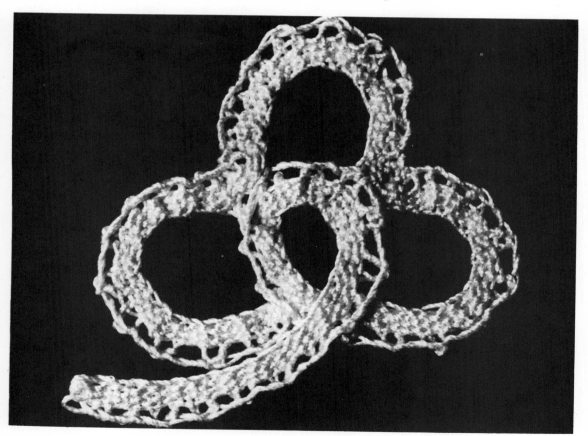

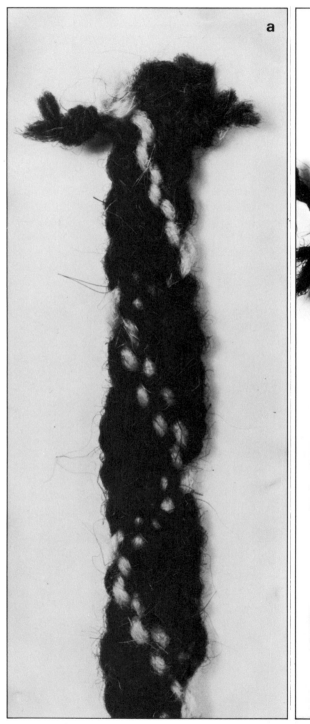

Finger weaving

The braids in **126a** and **b** also do not require
prickings. For **126a**, five pairs are pinned to the
pillow and each pair in turn is taken from left to
right, working whole stitch with every other pair
(**127**). With more threads and a little experimenting, patterns similar to those produced by finger
weaving can be formed (**126b**). These are compact
braids for which woollen threads are most suitable
– carpet thrums were used for both examples.

127 Working finger weaving

128 Narrow edgings

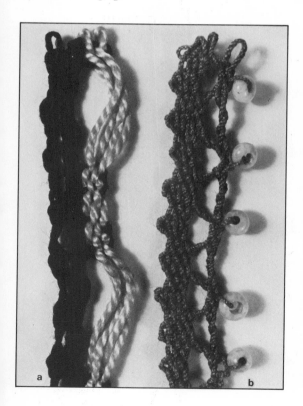

Narrow edgings

Two-colour edging

For the edging in **128a**, use pricking **78**, and 6 pairs
No 5 cotton perle: 2 prs black at each of A and B; 2
prs orange at C. Work as braid **76b**, but leave the
right-hand (orange) pairs loose – ie unplaited –
between pins 2 and 10, just taking them beside pins
at 4 and 5.

Beaded edging

For the edging in **128b**, use pricking **129**, and 5
pairs. Thread small beads onto one pair of
workers, hang at A; hang a second pair of workers
at C (No 20 crochet cotton). Hang 2 prs passives at
B, 1 pr at D (No 10 crochet cotton). Starting at the
left: *3 w st/(tw wks and pr from D) 3 times/w
st/tw wks 2 or 3 times/bring up a bead and pin to
1/tw wks/dbl with passives/tw wks 3 times. Leave.
Take the workers from C towards the left: 2 w
st/pin at 2/2 w st. Leave. With the first pair of
workers: 3 w st/pin at 3. Repeat from *.

129 Pricking for **128b**

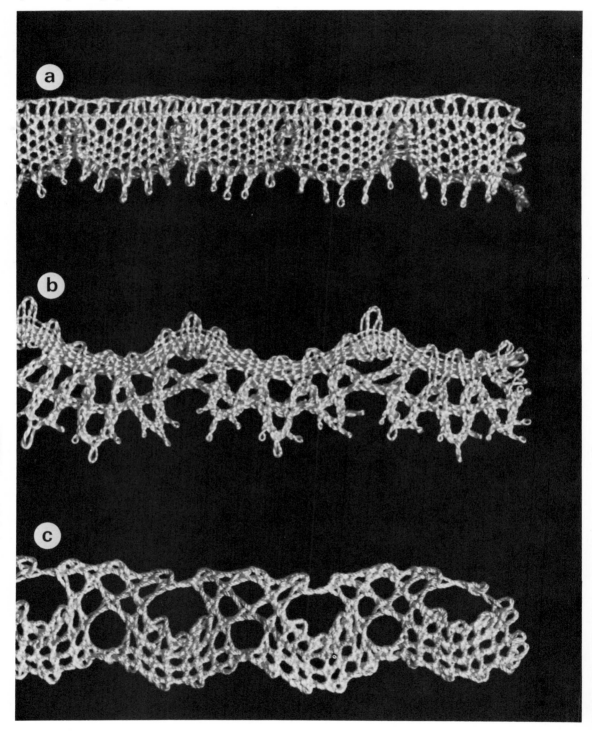

Butterfly motif worked in dyed linen thread with silver cording and sequins (see fig 221)

Child's poncho worked in double knitting wool (see fig 197)

(Top) Belt made of garden twine with wooden beads (see fig 186a); *(centre)* stretch belt in crochet cotton and black elastic (see fig 188); *(bottom)* tie belt in courtelle crêpe with beads (see fig 186b)

Scalloped edgings

Half stitch edging

For the edging in **130a**, use pricking **131**, and 7 pairs No 12 cotton perle, plus gimp thread hung to the right of the other threads. Most of the braid is half stitch. The left-hand edge is 'closed' with two twists before and after the pin, and one passive pair worked in doubles. On the right-hand edge a picot is worked outside the gimp.

The first row is therefore: twist 2nd pair from left twice/dbl/4 $\frac{1}{2}$ st/tw wks and pass gimp between/picot at 1. After working pin 10: take the gimp towards the left through 4 pairs, twist these

Scalloped plait and picot edging

Use pricking **132** for the edging in **130b**, and 8 pairs No 12 cotton perle: 4 prs at A; 2 prs at each of B and C. Work a whole stitch braid with the 4 pairs from A. Make a plait with the two pairs from B and another with the two pairs from C. 'Cross 4 pairs' at 3, 7, 10, 14, 17, 21 and 28. Make picots at 4, 5, 6, 11, 12 etc. Work one double between picots. 'Cross 3 pairs'/pin/'cross 3 pairs' at 1, 8, 15 and 22.

Three-colour edging

Use pricking **133** for the edging in **130c**, and 6 pairs No 20 crochet cotton: 1 pr red at A; 1 pr white at C; 2 prs yellow at each of B and D. The path of each pair is shown on the pricking. Work a double wherever two pairs cross.

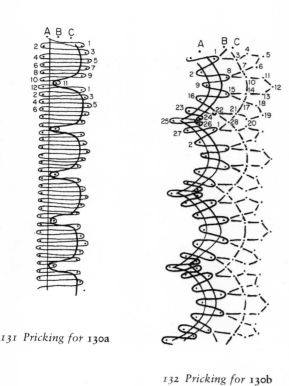

131 Pricking for 130a

132 Pricking for 130b

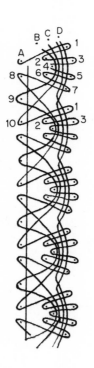

pairs. Take 2nd pair from left as workers: dbl with passives/pass gimp between workers/pin at 11/tw wks/pass gimp between wks then to the right through four pairs. Take workers back through to the left and continue with the braid.

133 Pricking for 130c

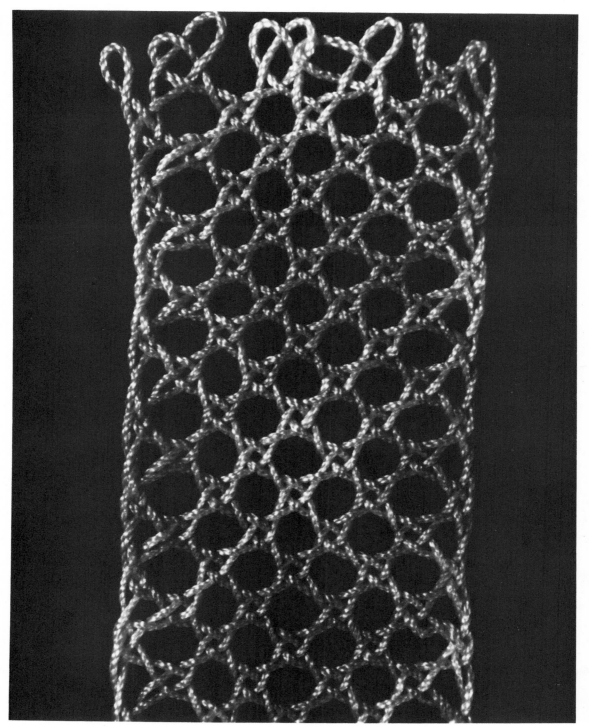

7 Torchon Lace

The patterns in this chapter are for narrow laces of the type known as Torchon. Interesting braids can be produced using two or more colours, although traditionally they are worked in one colour and used as edgings or insertion.

The basis of the lace is a square grid, and the patterns are easily drafted on squared paper: a 5 mm or $\frac{1}{4}$ in square is a useful size for No 20 crochet cotton, but a larger or smaller scale may be used. Pinholes are made in the centre of each square and at the corners – see pricking 135.

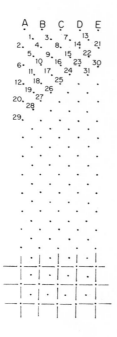

Torchon ground

Illustration 134, pricking 135, shows one of the simplest ways of using this grid. Use 10 pairs, and hang two pairs at each of the starting pins as follows: 2 prs red at A and E; 2 prs white at C; 1 pr white and 1 pr red at each of B and D.

As can be seen from the numbering on the pricking, the lace is worked diagonally. With 1 pr from A and 1 pr from B: $\frac{1}{2}$ st/pin at 1/$\frac{1}{2}$ st (**136**). With 1 pr from A and 1 pr from 1: dbl/pin at 2 beside the dbl. With 1 pr from B and 1 pr from C: $\frac{1}{2}$ st/pin at 3/$\frac{1}{2}$ st. With 1 pr from 1 and 1 pr from 3: $\frac{1}{2}$ st/pin at 4/$\frac{1}{4}$ st. Continue in this way with $\frac{1}{2}$ st/pin/$\frac{1}{2}$ st in the main part (5, 7, 8, 9 etc), and a double with the pin beside it at the edges (6, 12, 20, 21 etc).

A regular arrangement of stitches like this is called a 'ground'. Different grounds are produced by, for example, working doubles instead of half stitch, or putting in extra twists between stitches. The width of the ground may be varied by adding or taking away rows of squares – each additional row of squares requires two extra pairs of thread. Passive or gimp threads may be introduced into the ground, tallies may be worked at intervals, or the edge may be varied.

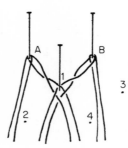

135 Pricking for Torchon ground using a 5 mm grid

136 First stitch in a Torchon ground

75

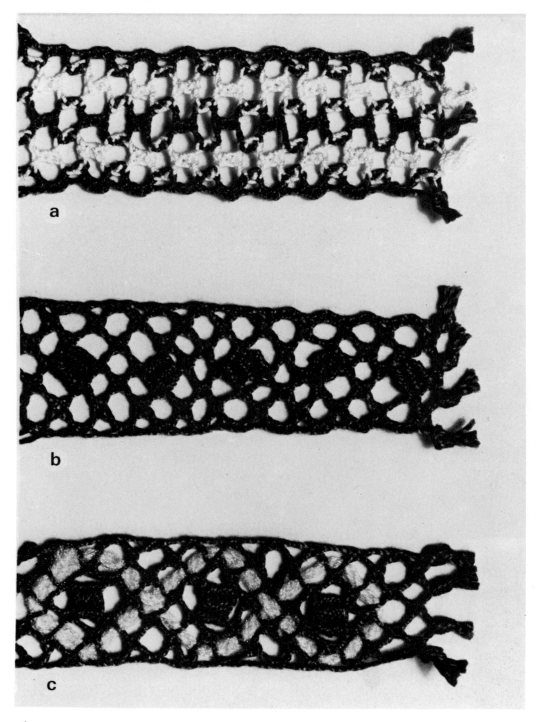

137 (a) Doubles ground; (b) half stitch ground with tallies; (c) tallies and gimp

Torchon ground variations

The three examples in **137**, each worked on a $\frac{1}{4}$ inch grid, show some of the possibilities of Torchon braid.

Doubles ground

Use pricking **138** for the braid in **137a**, and 10 pairs: 2 prs turquoise at each of A, C and E (No 8 cotton perle); 2 prs white at each of B and D (No 20 crochet cotton). This is a ground composed of doubles. The order of work is the same as in **134**, but one double (instead of a half stitch) is made before and one after every pin.

Half stitch ground with tallies

When working either **137b** or **137c** it is helpful to have the position of the tallies, and the gimp, marked on the pricking (see **139** and **141**), but three squares width of a plain grid (**138**) may be used. For **137b** use pricking **139**, and 8 pairs: 2 prs at each of A to D (No 8 cotton perle). Work a $\frac{1}{2}$ st/pin/$\frac{1}{2}$ st ground. (Note the order of the pins.) After pin 8, work the first tally as follows: use pairs from 3 and 6 to work a tally of six weavings (T14), finish with the threads in position to work $\frac{1}{2}$ st/pin/$\frac{1}{2}$ st at each of pins 9 and 10 (**140**). Work the second tally on the other diagonal.

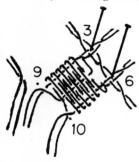

140 Working a tally in a ground

Half stitch ground with tallies and gimp

For **137c**, use pricking **141**, and 8 pairs (turquoise No 8 cotton perle): 2 prs hung at each of A to D. Plus one gimp pair (red Double Knitting Courtelle). For the ground: twist both pairs/$\frac{1}{2}$ st/pin/$\frac{1}{2}$ st (note order of pins). Gimp: after working pin 11 hang the gimp temporarily over pin 3. Work the next five pins (12 to 16) twisting each pair before passing the gimp between, then twisting again (**41c**). Remove pin 3. Tally: work a tally of eight weavings with pairs from 13 and 15.

Work the ground stitches at pins 17, 18 and 19. Pass gimps between other threads, twisting as before, then work pins 20, 21 etc. Cross the gimps before working the second diamond shape.

138 Pricking for Torchon ground using a $\frac{1}{4}$ inch grid

139 Pricking for 137b

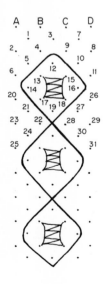

141 Pricking for 137c

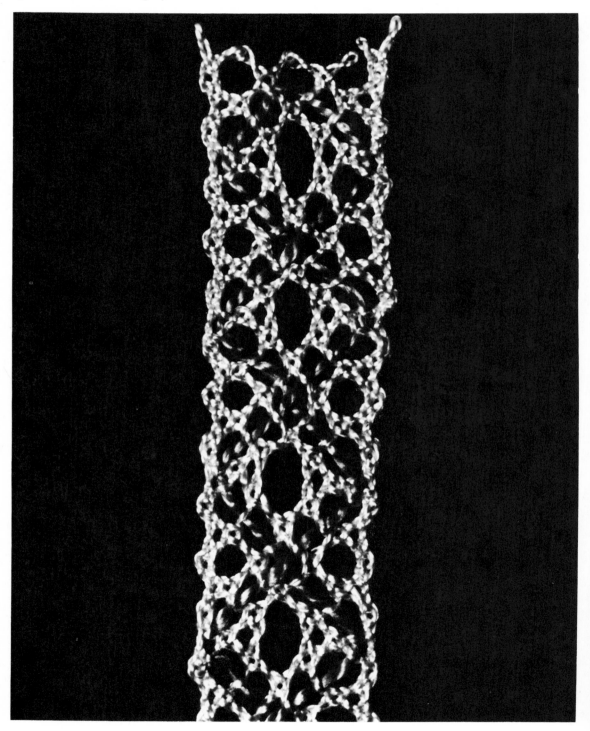

Braid with holes and gimp

The braid in **142** features small holes within gimp diamonds. Use pricking **143**, and 8 pairs (white No 12 cotton perle): 1 pr at each of A and E; 2 prs at each of B, C and D. Also use one gimp pair (orange No 8 cotton perle). To work the ground: $\frac{1}{2}$ st/pin/$\frac{1}{2}$ st. To work the edge: dbl/pin/dbl. Work the gimp as in **137c**. For the hole: work pins 9 to 13 ($\frac{1}{2}$ st/pin/$\frac{1}{2}$ st), then use pairs from 10 and 11 to work pin 14, and from 12 and 13 to work pin 15.

143 Pricking for 142

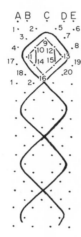

144 Braid with oval holes

Other interesting effects can be obtained by taking a gimp thread (or a line of cording) more or less at random through a Torchon ground.

Braid with oval holes

Braid **144** combines Torchon ground with a braid similar to **119b**. Use 12 pairs: 8 prs brown No 8 cotton perle – 3 prs at each of A and E, 2 prs at C; 4 prs orange No 20 crochet cotton – 2 prs at each of B and D. On each side work a single row of $\frac{1}{2}$ st/pin/$\frac{1}{2}$ st ground with dbl/pin/dbl at the edge. Work a whole stitch braid – with one pair brown as workers and two pairs of orange passives – on either side of the oval spaces. Connect the workers of the braid to the ground with dbl/pin/dbl. After working pin 30, cross over the two sets of passives and the workers as in **122**.

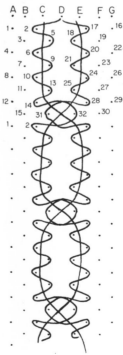

145 Pricking for 144

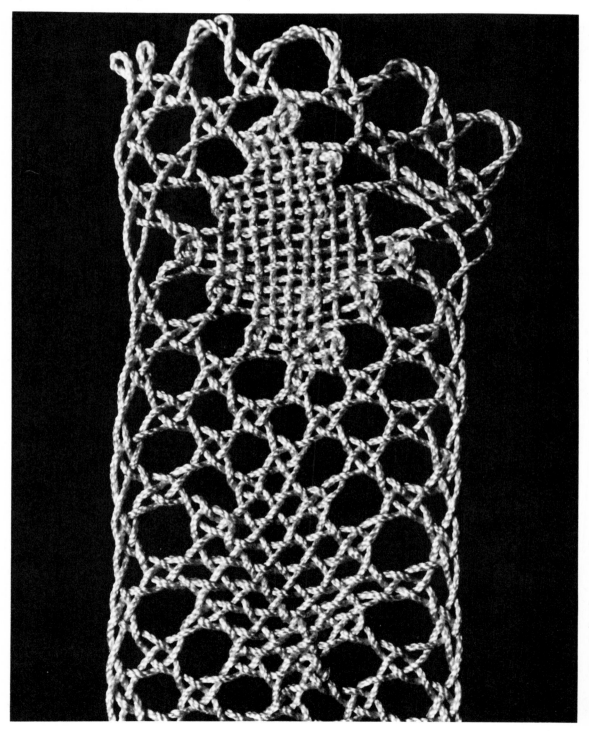

Grounds with whole stitch and half stitch diamonds

Panels of whole or half stitch may be used with the various grounds. These may be worked on a plain grid or on a specially marked pricking. For **146** use pricking **147**, and 10 pairs: 2 prs hung at each starting pin. Work a ground of $\frac{1}{2}$ st/pin/$\frac{1}{2}$ st until pin 12 is in place. Twist the pairs from 3 and 9, with them: w st/pin at 14/w st. Use the left-hand of these pairs as workers to work a diamond in whole stitch, taking in one pair (first twisted) at each of pins 14 to 19, and leaving out one pair at each of pins 18 to 23. This should leave two pairs to work the final w st/pin/w st at 24. Continue with the two triangles of ground.

Work the half stitch diamond in the same way. Unlike the half stitch braid it does not need to be bounded by doubles, so at each of pins 13 to 24 work $\frac{1}{2}$ st/pin/$\frac{1}{2}$ st.

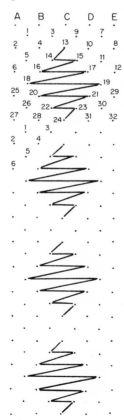

147 Pricking for 146

148 Pricking for 149

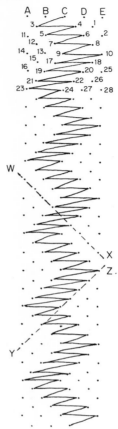

Torchon corner

Prickings for Torchon lace are relatively difficult to draft for curves, but a neat right angle can be made as follows. Finish the first length of braid on a diagonal. Tie the bobbins in groups and support their weight; remove all the pins. Turn the worked braid at right angles to the pricking and repin. Use planty of pins so this part does not become distorted – it may be necessary to make a few extra holes. Continue with the braid.

Illustration **149**, pricking **148**, shows such a corner. Use 10 pairs ('bold stitch'): 2 prs hung at each starting pin. This braid has a zigzag of half stitch running between triangles of $\frac{1}{2}$ st/pin/$\frac{1}{2}$ st ground. For the corner: work until pins are placed along the line W—X; remove the work from the pricking and repin with the last stitches along the line Y—Z.

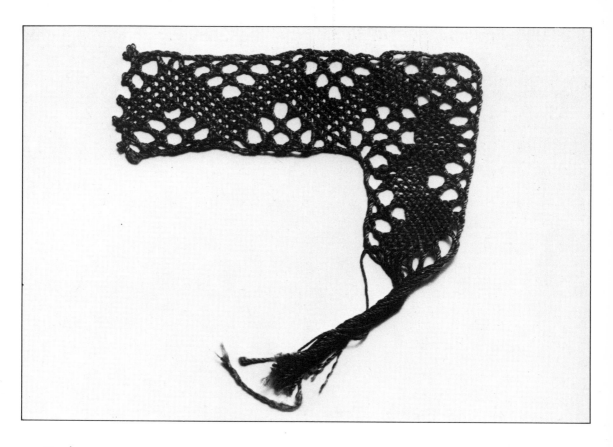

149 Torchon corner

T21: Spiders

A common feature of Torchon lace is the 'spider'. Worked in a diamond-shaped space in the ground, the spider may have eight or twelve 'legs' (occasionally more).

Twelve-legged spider

For a twelve-legged spider (**150a**), work the ground until pins are in the holes *a* to *i*. Twist the pairs from *b*, *c* and *d*, and *f*, *g* and *h* three times each – 6 legs. Working in w st: take the pair from *b* across those from *f*, *g* and *h*; then take the pairs from *c* and *d* across those from *f*, *g* and *h*.

Put in a pin (j) at the centre of the diamond – it will usually be necessary to pull firmly on all six pairs at this point (**152**). Still working in w st take each pair back to its original side. Twist each pair three times, then close the diamond by working pins *k* to *q*.

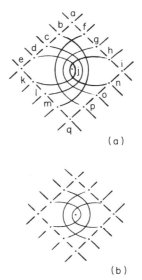

150 Prickings for spiders: (a) twelve-legged, (b) eight-legged

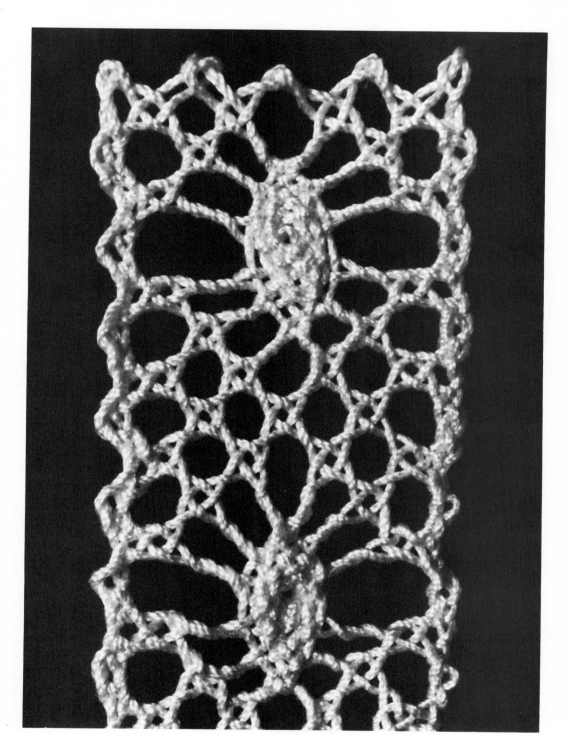

151 Spiders in torchon ground

83

152 A twelve-legged spider half worked

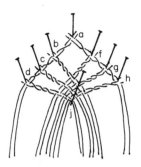

Eight-legged spider

Just four pairs are used for an eight-legged spider (**150b**), but the working is otherwise similar to that of the twelve-legged version.

Spider braid

Illustration **151**, worked on pricking **153** with 12 pairs No 20 crochet cotton, has twelve-legged spiders in a $\frac{1}{2}$ st/pin/$\frac{1}{2}$ st ground, with dbl/pin/dbl on the edge.

Fan sampler

Another common feature of Torchon lace is the 'fan' edging. Illustration **154**, pricking **155**, shows a sampler of fans using whole stitch, half stitch or doubles, worked between triangles of ground. Use 9 pairs: 2 prs at each of A, B and C; 3 prs at D.

Start with a small triangle of ground worked with the pairs from A and B and one pair from C. After pin 6 use the other pair from C as workers to make the fan. Take in a pair from the ground at 8, 10, 12 and 14, and leave one pair out of the fan at 14, 16, 18 and 20.

The stitches used in the sampler are as follows. Fans: (**a**) whole stitch; (**b**) doubles; (**c**) half stitch with doubles on the outer edge; (**d**) whole stitch with doubles on the edge, separated by twists in the workers; (**e**) as (**c**) with a tally worked in the centre of the fan after working pin 14; (**f**) whole stitch, edge pair twisted, workers twisted to the left of three passive pairs.

The grounds are: (1) $\frac{1}{2}$ st/pin/$\frac{1}{2}$ st; (2) w st/pin/w st; (3) dbl/pin/dbl; (4) as (1) with an extra twist between pins; (5) twist both pairs/$\frac{1}{2}$ st/pin/twist both pairs/$\frac{1}{2}$ st.

153 Pricking for **151**

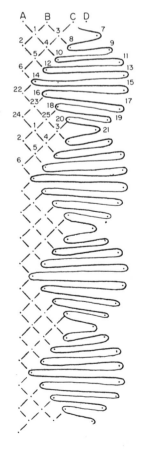

154 Pricking for fans

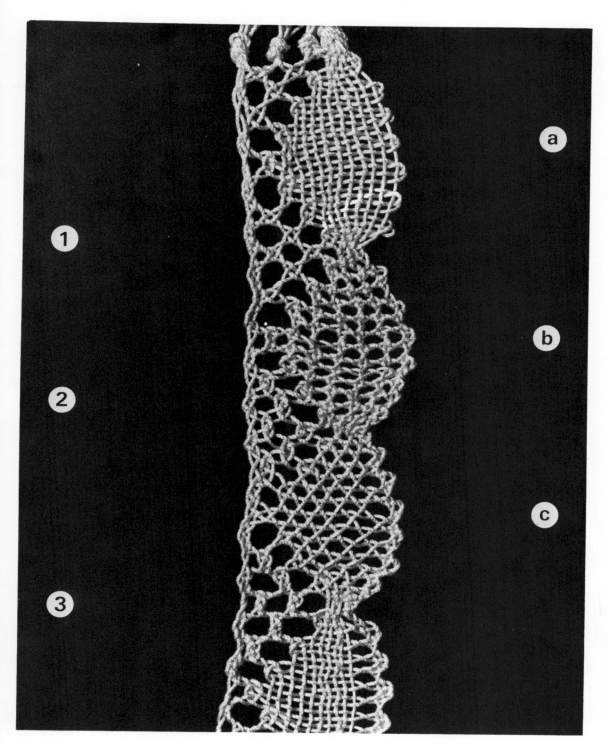

155 (a) Fan sampler

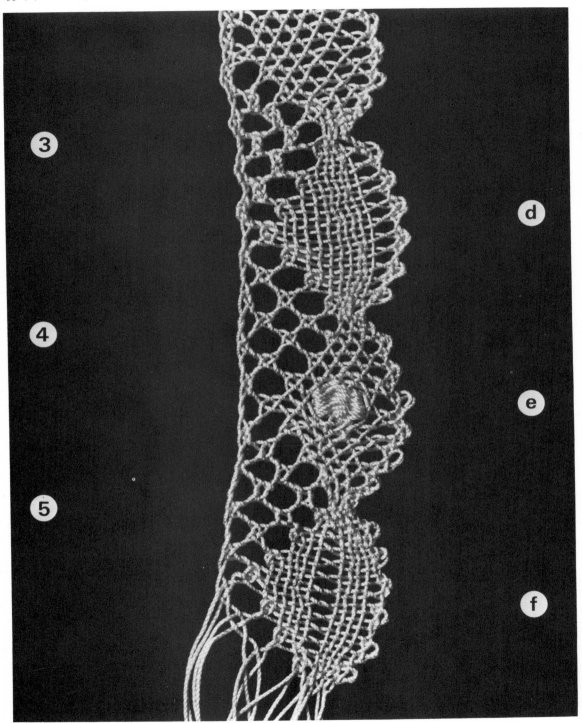

8 Additional Techniques

The braids described in the previous chapters may be worked as lengths, then applied as decorative strips, folding or gathering (**156**), and cutting where required – the cut end should be stitched, or a small amount of glue applied. However, neater results will usually be obtained by shaping the braid on the pillow. The notes and techniques described in this chapter show how this may be done.

156 Shaping a straight braid: (a) folding,
(b) gathering

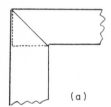 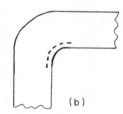

157 Starting with a fringe

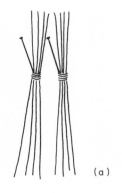

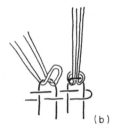

Starting

The method of starting described in T8 – ie with bobbins wound in pairs – is the most generally useful, particularly where the two ends of the braid are to be joined (see the notes below on finishing). The other methods described here are useful for specific purposes.

Fringed

Either knot groups of threads some distance from the ends, and pin through the knots (**157a**); or start as T8, but leave the loops, and into them knot short lengths of thread (**157b**).

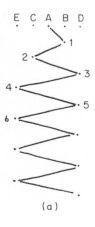

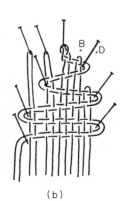

158 Tapered start

Tapered

Use a pricking as in **158a**. Hang two pairs at A, one pair at each of B to E. Work a double with the two pairs at A. Now work in whole stitch bringing in one extra pair – from B, C, D and E – before each of pins 1, 2, 3 and 4. After pin 6 remove the pins from B, C, D and E and gently pull the passives to eliminate the loops (**158b**). Whole stitch is used here, but other stitches could be used.

Fixed

Illustration **159** shows threads looped onto a clasp for the start of a belt. In **160** the threads are 'sewn' in pairs (**160a**) or groups (**160b**) to the edge of a braid.

159 Fixing threads to a clasp

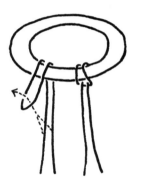

160 'Sewing' threads to the edge of a braid

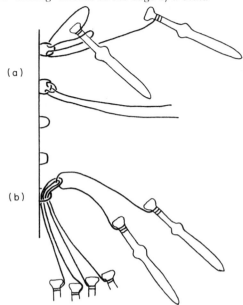

(a)

(b)

Starting two braids together

Wind the bobbins in pairs and lay the threads across the pillow. Put in a central pin and extra pins to keep the threads in order (**161a**). The two top threads, or the bottom two, on each side will be the workers. Illustration **161b** shows one row of whole stitch worked on one side. (See also the instructions for starting the tie in chapter 9.)

To start two braids of different colours link two threads as in **161c** before laying them across the pillow.

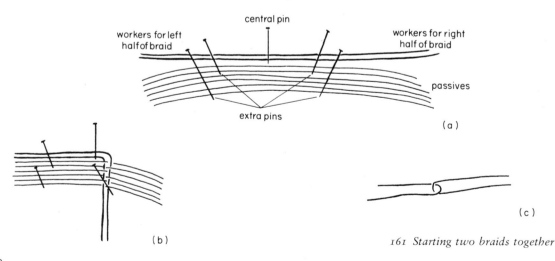

workers for left half of braid

central pin

workers for right half of braid

passives

extra pins

(a)

(b)

(c)

161 Starting two braids together

Finishing

At the end of some pieces the threads may simply be tied in pairs or groups and cut off, either close to the work or to leave a fringe. On other items a sewing needle will be needed to make a neat finish as illustrated in **162**. Ends darned back into the braid should follow the lines of worked threads (**162a**). Two ends of braid may be joined by darning alternate threads into the start and finish (**162b**). Do check before joining that the braid is not twisted. 'Sewings' can be made (**162c**) to connect a last loop of braid to the first before joining the ends as in **b**.

Keeping the work pinned to the pillow while darning will reduce distortion. Darn in all the threads before trimming the ends. Some of the threads may be discarded before the end of the braid to make the finish less bulky – see T23 below. If the braid is to be mounted on fabric, the ends can often be darned into the mount.

162 Finishing

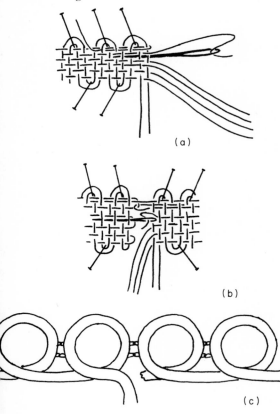

(a)

(b)

(c)

T22: Adding extra threads

Wind a pair of bobbins and hang over a convenient pin; put the bobbins into the required position (**163a**). Work the new threads into the braid for two or three rows then remove the pin and gently pull the bobbins to eliminate the loop (**163b**).

163 Adding threads

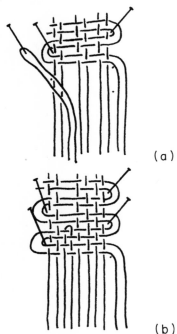

(a)

(b)

T23: Reducing the number of threads

Put unwanted bobbins to the back of the pillow. Continue with the braid for several rows then trim threads close to the work. The threads should usually be discarded in pairs and only one pair per row (**164**).

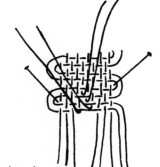

164 Discarding threads

Shaping

The use of turning stitches and 'sewings' to shape curved and angled braids was described in chapter 5. When a corner is required for an otherwise straight braid a special pricking will be needed. Make corner prickings with several rows of straight braid on either side.

Prickings for curves

Place pinholes along the outside of curves at normal spacing. On the inner edge put the holes closer together (**165a**) or, if the curve is tight, omit some or all of the pins and work turning stitches (**165b**). Arrange that turning stitches are made with pairs of the same colour, for example if the edge pair contrasts with the rest of the braid make turning stitches with one of the passives. If this is not possible make one pinhole on the inside of the curve, on each row place a pin temporarily in this hole, removing it when the workers return to the outer edge. Use the one pinhole as often as necessary to round the curve (**165c**). Keep the braid flat by pulling firmly on the inside pairs and omitting twists.

Prickings for angles

A right angle for a narrow braid may be made as in **104**. For a wider braid two or more turning stitches will be needed on either side of the angle (**166a**). A method which results in a change of worker is shown in **166b**. More turning stitches, made with passives nearer the outside of the angle, are needed for an acute angle (**166c**). Angles worked on these prickings are illustrated in **167**.

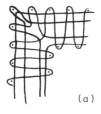

(a)

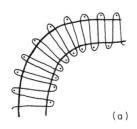

(a)

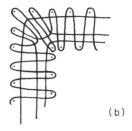

(b)

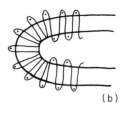

(b)

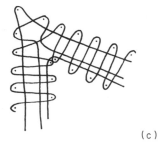

(c)

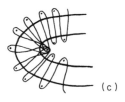

(c)

165 Prickings for curves

166 Prickings for angles

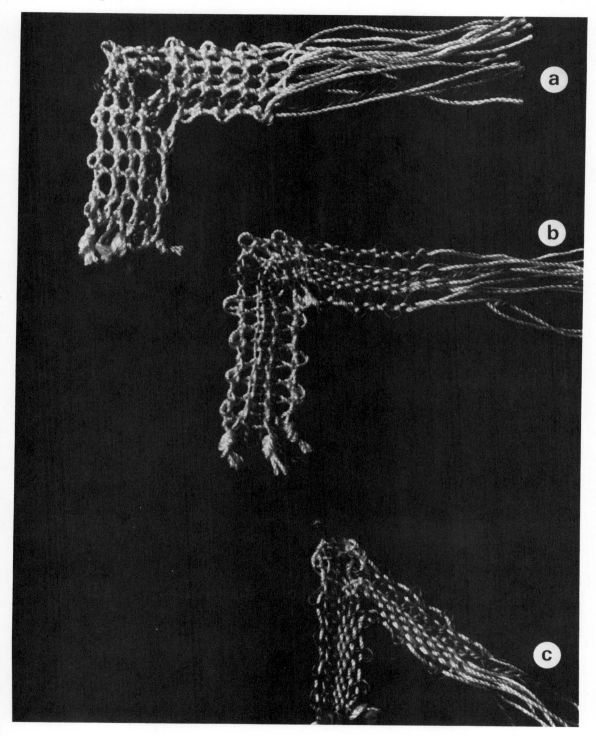

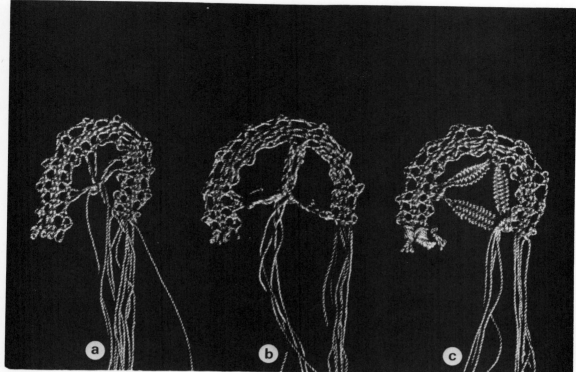

169 Worked fillings

Changing prickings

When transferring a partly worked braid, support the weight of the bobbins (held in groups with elastic bands, or pinned into a cover cloth – see 33) while the pins are removed, the new pricking fixed to the pillow and the braid pinned in place. There should be sufficient room on the new pricking to allow several rows of the worked braid to be held with pins.

Use of a flat pillow

When working a design where the braid frequently changes direction it is usually easier to work on a flat pillow. Use two cover cloths so both worked and unworked portions of the pricking are covered (168). Push pins well down before covering.

T24: Fillings

Shaping a braid will often produce a space that can be filled in one of the ways illustrated in 169, worked on the prickings in 170.

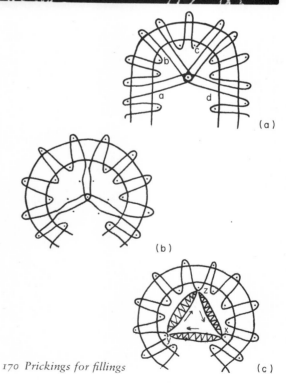

170 Prickings for fillings

93

Using pricking **170a**, at *a*, *b* and *c* twist the workers eight times, take them round a central pin and back into the braid. From *d* twist the workers four times and 'sew' through all three loops at the central pin (see **98**), twist four times and take back into the braid. Vary the number of twists and arms of the star according to the size of space and the effect desired.

Using pricking **170b**, for a larger space, or more solid effect, plait workers and edge pair and take round a central pin. When the plait returns to the braid, 'sew' one pair to the first double of the plait. 'Sew' the last plait through all the loops at the centre, treating the four threads as one pair. Plaits may be ornamented with picots.

Using pricking **170c**, work the braid until the space is nearly enclosed then use workers and edge pair from *x* to work three leaf-shaped tallies. Make 'sewings' (treating the four threads as one pair) between tallies at *y* and *z*, and at the start of

the first tally.

Fillings can also be worked with extra threads 'sewn' to the edge of the completed braid (**160**), but there will then be the problem of the additional ends to darn in (**171**).

171 Extra threads added for a filling

172 Joining braids with (a) a needle, (b) a crochet hook

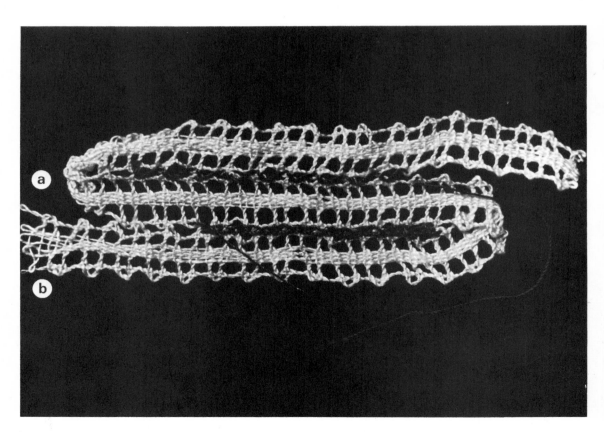

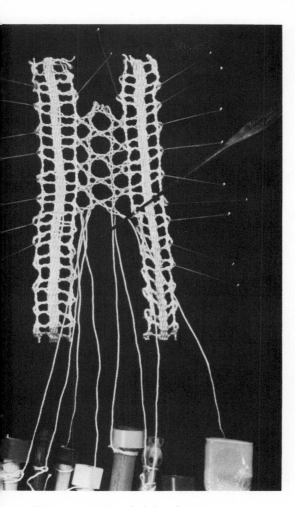

173 Using 'sewings' to link braids

Joining braids

Braids can be worked separately then joined with
needle and thread (**172a**) or a crochet chain (**172b**).
Alternatively the braids may be linked as they are
worked. One method is to work a complete braid
and then pin it alongside the pricking for the next:
work this braid making 'sewings' where the two
braids touch – illustration **173** shows two braids
being linked by the working of a third.

A second method is to make a pricking that
includes all the braids: work all the braids together; wherever two braids touch, work dbl/pin/
dbl ·(or w st/pin/w st) with the two pairs of
workers (see braid **80a**). One disadvantage is that
a large number of bobbins is required.

T25: Applying beads with 'sewings'

This technique is used to mount beads between
two braids or in a braid with two pairs of workers.

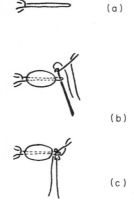

174 Applying beads on picots

One method is to work one braid making picots
where beads are required – the picots must be long
enough to take the chosen beads (**174a**). Work the
second braid using a crochet hook to pull the
picots through the beads. Make 'sewings' to these
loops with workers of the second braid (**174b** and
c).

An alternative method is to work both parts of
the braid(s) until a bead is required. Twist both
pairs of workers. Use a crochet hook to pull one
thread through the bead. Pass one bobbin of the
other worker pair through the loop (**175a**). Twist
both pairs and pull tight (**175b**).

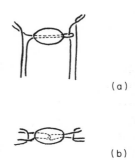

175 Applying beads on workers

95

Mounting

On fabric backgrounds, mount braids as appliqués, edgings or insertions, using small stitches that pass through the holes left by the pins. On firm surfaces adhesives can be used. The use of a glue that will wash out of fabric will allow the braid to be removed later and re-used, otherwise choose a transparent craft glue. Apply sparingly using a pin for fine work.

Threads

Although, with care, most types of thread can be used, some will present particular problems in working.

Very fine thread

This thread is liable to snap. If it does so, rejoin the bobbin as if it were newly wound (30). If the break is close to the work either undo a little to allow the double thread to be worked, or be prepared to darn in the broken ends.

Very thick thread

Normal bobbins may prove too thin and light. Try dolly-pegs (wooden clothes pins (pegs) with round heads), or dispense with bobbins and wind the thread into a 'butterfly' (176).

176 Thread 'butterfly'

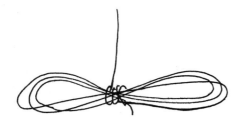

Textured thread

If it is difficult to pull stitches into position keep a crochet hook or strong pin handy to ease the threads into place.

Springy thread

If the hitch will not stay under the head of the bobbin try two hitches or a small elastic band.

'Elastic' thread

An even tension is difficult to achieve with threads that stretch easily (eg shirring elastic, some synthetic yarns) – pull the threads just hard enough to position the stitches.

Metallic thread

Flat lurex threads tend to become very twisted in use – rotate the bobbins at intervals to untwist. Another type of thread has a metallic covering over a thin cotton or synthetic cord. This covering cracks easily, so it is usually more satisfactory to use the threads as passives or gimps – where twisting and rubbing are minimal – than as workers.

Dyeing thread

Thread in loose hanks may be home-dyed, and shaded effects can be obtained by tie-dyeing. This involves tying the hank into knots or binding it with string at intervals to prevent the dye from reaching all parts of the hank, thus producing an attractive partially-coloured effect.

Calculating lengths

It is difficult to estimate the amount of thread to wind on each bobbin: passives need be only slightly longer than the finished braid if the thread is thin, but workers, weavers of tallies, etc, need to be considerably longer. Fresh threads may however be readily added (see 30), or if a worker bobbin is nearly emptied when nearing the end of a piece it is often possible to exchange it – by putting in an extra twist (177a) or cross (177b) – for a passive bobbin containing more thread.

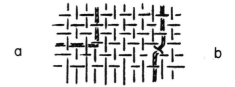

177 Changing pairing of threads: (a) extra twist, (b) extra cross

Experimenting with thread

Use oddments of thread – eg the ends left on bobbins after working several pieces – to experiment with different combinations of colour and texture. It is not always necessary to use a pricking: work directly on the pillow, or over squared paper or a rough sketch.

Designing prickings

The designing of prickings is not particularly difficult, although considerable patience will be required to position all the pinholes on a pattern involving many curves and crossings – in such a case it may be more satisfactory to outline the pattern on paper, cover with tracing film, then place the pins as seems most appropriate while the braid is being worked.

Modifying an existing pricking is often easier than starting from scratch. Working on squared paper is usually helpful. Designing a straight braid should cause few problems. For more complex patterns use the following procedure.

(1) Select the type or types of braid to be used, noting the following points.

(a) The more complex the route to be taken by the braid, the simpler the braid should be.

(b) The nature of the braid may be changed in the course of the work, for example by working an open braid along straight stretches, reverting to basic braid on the curves.

(c) A different braid may be added as an edging using one of the methods shown in 172 or 173.

(2) Make a full-scale sketch marking the course of the braid or braids.

(3) Mark the position of pinholes on the outside of curves, then those on the inside – omitting some where necessary. Draw the route to be taken by the workers.

(4) Before completing stage 3, trace off a small part of the pattern and work some of the chosen braid. This will give the opportunity of checking that the appropriate number and thickness of threads have been selected. If the braid does not seem right, try altering one (or more) of the following:

(a) the number of passives
(b) the spacing of pinholes
(c) the width of the braid
(d) the thickness of the thread.

(5) Decide on fillings for any spaces, mark their positions.

(6) Trace the complete pattern onto architect's tracing film (pin the film to the pillow over plain paper), or prick through onto card and copy the markings (T16). A clear original sketch can be used as the pricking with a covering of tracing film for strength.

Large designs

If the design is too large to fit on the pillow make the pricking in sections, each one overlapping the next. When one section has been worked, transfer to the overlap at the start of the next section, pin in place and continue.

9 Trimmings, Motifs and Accessories

Trimmings

A number of suggestions for using braids as trimmings are illustrated in **178**. The lampshade can be trimmed with two lengths of the braid shown in illustration **51**, using maroon tallies on green to pick up the colouring of Regency-style curtains. The beach skirt can have a contrast band of the braid in **86c**, gathered slightly for the corners. The edging of the dress yoke looks effective with the braid in **100b** with worked corners (pricking **102**). The basic braid trimming the child's trousers can be worked partly on pricking **17**, and partly on a ring-shaped pricking. A slightly sculptured effect for a picture frame can be given by two pieces of braid **45a** worked together on waved prickings, as sketched in **178**.

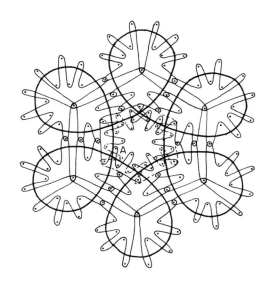

179 Pricking for 180

178 Braids as trimmings

Simple motifs

The three motifs in **180**, **181** and **183** illustrate the fillings described in T24.

Flower of six petals

Use pricking **179** for the motif in **180**, and 6 pairs: 4 prs No 20 crochet cotton – passives; 1 pr perle glitter – cable; 1 pr machine twist – workers. Start at A where the join will be hidden by the final curve. Work a whole stitch braid with a cable in the centre (T13a). Twist workers two or three times at the edge of the braid and about twelve times in the centre of the petals (T24a). Make 'sewings' where appropriate. Remove the motif from the pillow and finish by knotting or darning the ends into the starting loops.

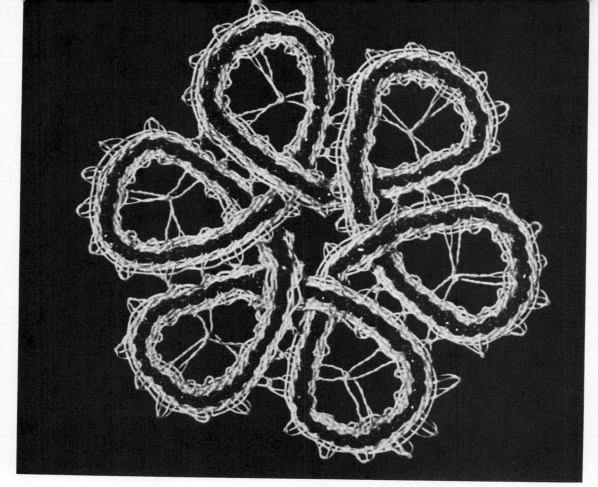

180 Flower with six petals

Trefoil

Use pricking **182** for the motif in **181**, and 9 pairs machine twist: 3 prs white; 6 prs pink. Hang on 2 prs white (as edge pairs) and 5 prs pink at A to work a basic braid. Use the edge pair and workers (from B, C etc) to work the filling T24b with two

doubles on each section of plait. Use T22 to hang on the last two pairs (one white, one pink) at D for a plaited edging as in **72**. Work four doubles for each plait except between G and H, and J and K, where you should work just two doubles. Make 'sewings' where appropriate, and turning stitches at I and L. This motif is suitable for use as a handkerchief corner.

181 Trefoil

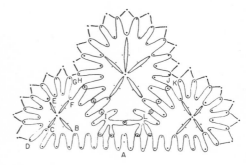

182 Pricking for 181

183 Quatrefoil

Quatrefoil

Use pricking **184** for the motif in **183**, and 6 pairs
machine twist: 1 pr black; 5 prs white. Start at A.
Work braid **34c** (ie $\frac{1}{2}$ st with doubles at the edge) to
D. Take out two pairs to work a triangle of three
tallies, make 'sewings' at B and C and back into
the braid at D (filling T24c). Continue in $\frac{1}{2}$ st.
Make a 'sewing' at E, and turning stitches on the
inside of curves.

For the edging, work braid **84a** with five pairs.
'Sew' to each leaf at F, G, H and I. Make picots
with two turns round the pin and extra twists
before and after.

184 Pricking for 183

Belts

If worked with suitable materials, most types of braid can be made into belts.

Half-belt

Four long strips of fabric will make a belt or half-belt (**185**). Fold and stitch the strips to conceal the raw edges, then plait (T2) as a trim for a dress. No bobbins are needed.

185 Half belt

187 Pricking for **186a**

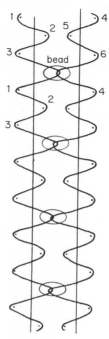

186 Two belts

Child's belt with a buckle

Pricking **158** is used to make the belt in **186a**. Use the following materials: 6 pairs garden twine; small buckle; 14 wooden beads – 7 threaded on each worker. Start as in **158**. Continue in whole stitch. Push up one bead in the middle of the twelfth, then on every sixth row. To finish, fold the end of the braid round the buckle, then darn in the ends of twine.

Tie belt

Pricking **187** is used for the belt in **186b**. Use the following materials: 6 pairs courtelle crêpe; small curtain ring; 30–36 beads. Start by fastening the threads onto the curtain ring as in **159**. Work two narrow braids in doubles – 2 prs passives, 1 pr workers for each. Use T25b to attach beads between the two braids. To finish, when the belt is the right length for the waist, plait each group of six threads for about 25 cm (10 in), discarding two or three threads part way. Thread a bead onto the end of each plait and knot the threads below it. Trim the tassels.

Stretch belt

Use pricking **189** for the belt in **188**, and the following materials: 16 pairs No 20 crochet cotton (4 prs white – workers; 12 prs contrast – passives); narrow black elastic (6 cord); one clasp 2·5 cm (1 in) wide. Use the method in **159** to fix the threads on one half of the clasp in this order: 3 prs passives/2 prs workers/6 prs passives/2 prs workers/3 prs passives. Work the belt as four braids each linked to adjacent braids on every row. For the link, work dbl/pin/dbl with the two pairs of workers (see **83**). Braids can be doubles, or whole stitch, or some of each.

189 Pricking for 188

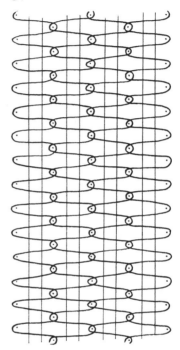

188 Stretch belt

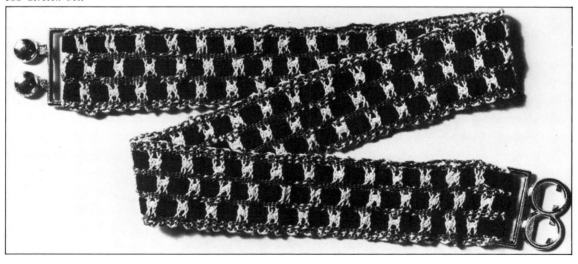

When the belt is a few centimetres (an inch) longer than the finished length required, cut off the threads and sew onto the second part of the clasp. Thread elastic between the braids and fasten at each end.

If the correct number of bobbins (16 prs) is not available: work half the belt with 8 pairs, then work the second half making 'sewings' along the centre (see 173).

Tie

Use prickings 121 and 190 to make the tie in 191. Use 8 pairs No 20 crochet cotton. To start, with the bobbins wound in pairs, hang the passives (6 pairs) over a pin at A on pricking 191, and workers (2 pairs) over B. Take one thread from each pair to work a whole stitch braid from 1 to 5 – twist workers at the pins. Use the other threads for the second half of the braid (see 161). After pin 10, remove pins A and B and pull the passives gently to shape the top of the ring. Work thirteen rings of 119b, then three progressively larger rings using a separate pricking – this is easily drafted on squared paper.

To finish, darn the passives into the opposite sides of the braid. On each side take one pair nearly to the top of the ring, one pair half way and one pair just a few stitches before cutting off. Cut off workers after a few darning stitches across the braid.

190 Tie

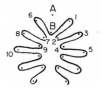

191 Starting the tie motif

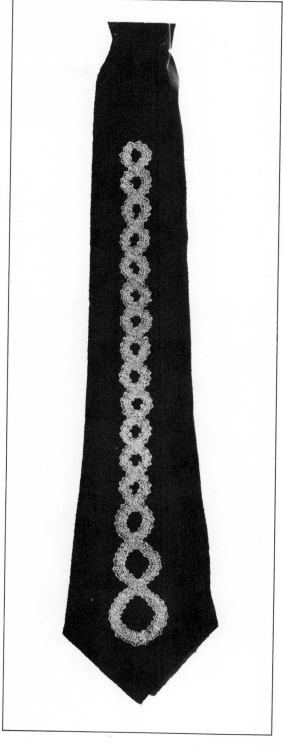

Household items

In addition to the more obvious household items such as table and tray cloths, aprons, lampshades etc, there are many small objects that may be decorated with braids or lace.

Lavender sachets

Two suggestions for lavender sachets are sketched in **192**. The square sachet below is edged with braid **76a**, worked on a pricking slightly smaller in scale than **77** and including corners, using three shades of machine twist. The heart shape above has an edging of **130c**, gathered on the inside edge to take it round the curves.

192 Lavender bags

193 Decorated jar

Decorated jar

Illustration **193** shows a thick green-tinted jam-jar given interest as a flower container by the application of two bands of braid. Two lengths of braid **109** were worked on pricking **105**, each with 3 pairs of yellow and 4 pairs of red No 20 crochet cotton. The second length was linked by 'sewings' to the angles of the first.

Other jars could be decorated as candle holders, or to hold sweets, etc, as gifts. Before starting the braid, measure the circumference of the jar, and check that a whole number of repeats can be worked – most braids can be stretched slightly. A small amount of craft glue will hold the finished braid in place.

Paperweight

The central motif in illustration **194** is in tenstick (**125**) worked with four pairs machine twist and a contrast gimp. The six-pointed star is made up of two separate triangles worked in whole stitch (see **80b**) with 2 pairs of workers and 4 pairs of passives (No 8 cotton perle). Seven sequins complete the design, which is glued on a backing card and placed under the glass dome.

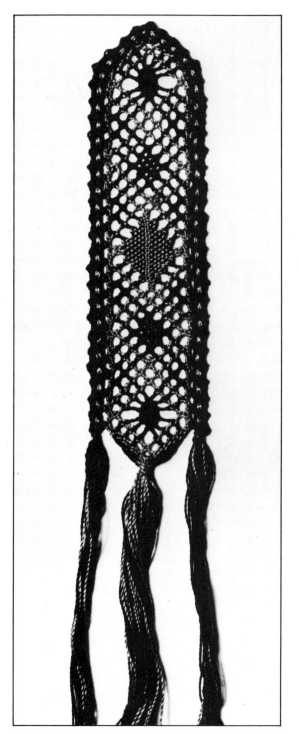

Bookmarks

Torchon bookmark

Trial pieces and samplers can often be turned into attractive bookmarks if consideration is given to the start and finish. In the first example (**195**), 12 pairs were used for a panel of Torchon ground with twelve-legged spiders, small half stitch diamonds and a larger whole stitch diamond. At the end of the panel, each pair in turn, starting at the outside, was brought to the centre in whole stitch. Two pairs were tied tightly round the rest to form a tassel.

The method employed in **161** was used to start the two lengths of braid **109** (6 prs in each) for the edging, which was 'sewn' to the edge of the Torchon panel, and each end was finished with a tassel. Cotton perle No 8 was used. For the Torchon panel, 6 prs navy and 6 prs blue were used, and for the edging, 10 prs navy and 2 prs blue.

Half stitch bookmark

The outline of the second bookmark (**196**) is half stitch with doubles on the outer edge. The various fillings were worked with threads 'sewn' to the inner edge (as in **172**). Five pairs of bobbins, each bobbin wound with one lurex thread and one cotton perle No 8, were used for the half stitch. The two types of thread were separated for the fillings.

195 Torchon bookmark

196 Half stitch bookmark with fillings

197 Poncho

Poncho

Alternate bands of straight and waved braids make an interesting fabric for a scarf, stole or poncho. The child's poncho in **197** is made of two 40 cm (16 in) long pieces, each composed of four straight and three waved braids. Each braid has a contrast chain as in **109**. Make it from the following materials: four 20 gm balls of double knitting wool in the main colour; small ball of contrasting wool. Seven pairs are needed for each braid – 6 prs main colour, 1 pr contrast – with an additional pair, wound with two thicknesses, for the fringe. Follow the order of working given below, using pricking **198**.

(1) On part A of the pricking, work a basic braid for the required length.

(2) On part B, work braid **100c**. Make 'sewings' to the first braid.

(3) Work a fringed braid (see **64**) on part C using the outer pinholes. Make 'sewings' to the waved braid.

(4) Remove the three braids from the pricking.

(5) Make a second panel of three braids this time using the inner pinholes on part C. Remove from the pricking.

(6) Pin a panel on each side of the pricking covering parts A and C.

(7) Connect the two panels by working a waved braid on part B and making 'sewings' (see **173**).

(8) Tie the threads in pairs and cut off for the fringe.

(9) Work a second piece of seven braids.

(10) Join the two pieces by sewing along a/b and c/d (**199**).

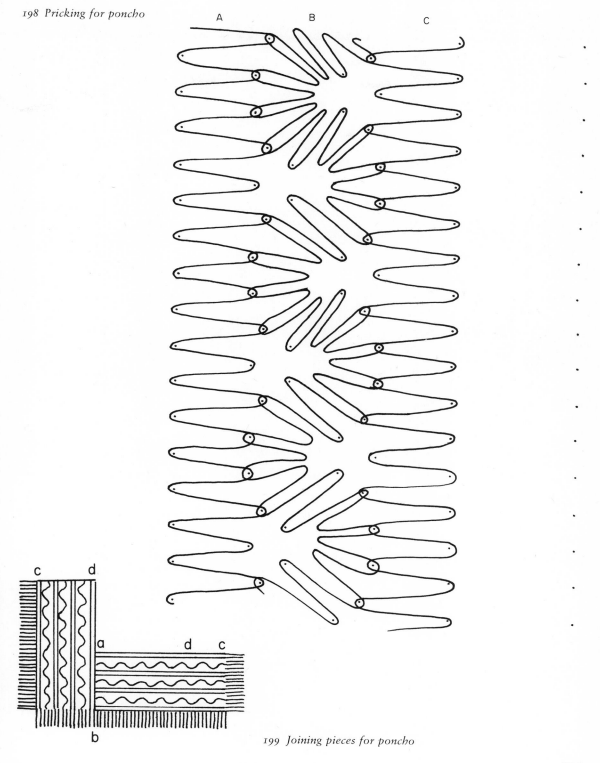

198 *Pricking for poncho*

199 *Joining pieces for poncho*

200 Baby's dress yoke

Yoke for a baby's dress

Use pricking **201** to make the yoke in **200**. The yoke section of a paper dress pattern gave the outline shape for this design which will fit a child of about six months. The pricking is for one half of the yoke – reverse the tracing for the second half. Use 9 pairs: 7 prs No 20 crochet cotton (orange); 2 prs No 5 cotton perle (orange). Start at A, finish at an equivalent point on the second half. Work basic braid on the curved inner sections and braid **111** on the straighter outside portions. Make 'sewings' where appropriate. Work fillings of tallies or twisted workers where indicated (or use plaits if preferred).

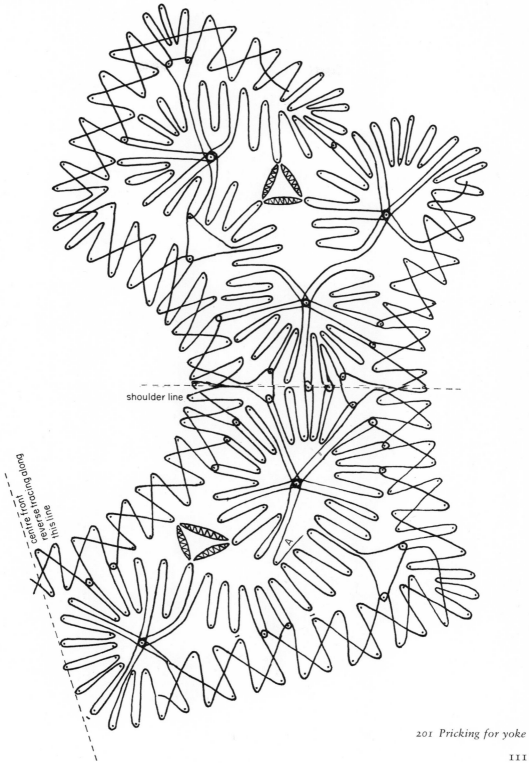

shoulder line

centre front
reverse tracing along
this line

A

201 Pricking for yoke

Shoulder bag

Use pricking 203 to work the bag in illustration 202.

Materials

Use carpet thrums in two shades of green (or double knitting wool); lining fabric – two pieces approximately 25 cm ×75 cm (10 in × 30 in); fastener (button, Velcro or press stud).

202 *Shoulder bag*

First side

Work four strips of Torchon ground (**134**) with eight-legged spiders (**150b**) on pricking **203a**. Twist three times at the outside pins – there is no edge pair. For each strip use 8 dark pairs and 4 light pairs, hanging the light at B, D, I and K. (When using thrums each length of wool is enough for one bobbin for one strip – about eight spiders – so knot pairs of thread for the start.)

Work the first strip – four light and four dark spiders – and finish by knotting threads in groups of four to make a fringe. Work a second strip 'sewing' it to the first along one edge (**173**), then add the third and fourth strips.

Second side

Work five strips of Torchon ground with tallies (**137b**) on pricking **203b**. Work the tallies with a double at the start and finish and five weavings. For three of the strips use 4 light pairs and 4 dark pairs. For the other two strips use 8 dark pairs, start these strips with 4 extra rows of ground (4 rows of pins) to stagger the tallies. Link the strips by 'sewings' and finish with a fringe as on the first side. Complete the side with two narrow strips of ground worked with 4 dark pairs.

Handle

Use 5 pairs to work about 130 cm (50 in) of the braid in **126a**.

Making up

Stitch the end portions of the handle to the edges of the side pieces to form gussets. Stitch through the knots of the fringe to close the bottom of the bag. Make up the lining using a narrow french seam. Bring the top over to the outside to enclose the starting knots with a neat hem. Attach the fastener, then trim the fringe.

(a)

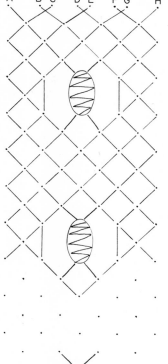

(b)

203 Prickings for shoulder bag

Evening purse

Use pricking 204 to make the motif for the purse in 205. Use the following materials: 5 pairs No 12 cotton perle – white; 1 pair gold lurex thread; a packet of small glass beads; a purse clip, mounting fabric and lining (or made-up fabric purse). Start at any point on the motif where the braid crosses itself. Use basic braid without an edge pair on the inside, place the lurex threads as first and last passives. Thread beads on the workers, push one up in the centre of every third row omitting portions where the braid crosses itself. Sew the finished motif to the fabric before making up the purse.

204 *Pricking for purse*

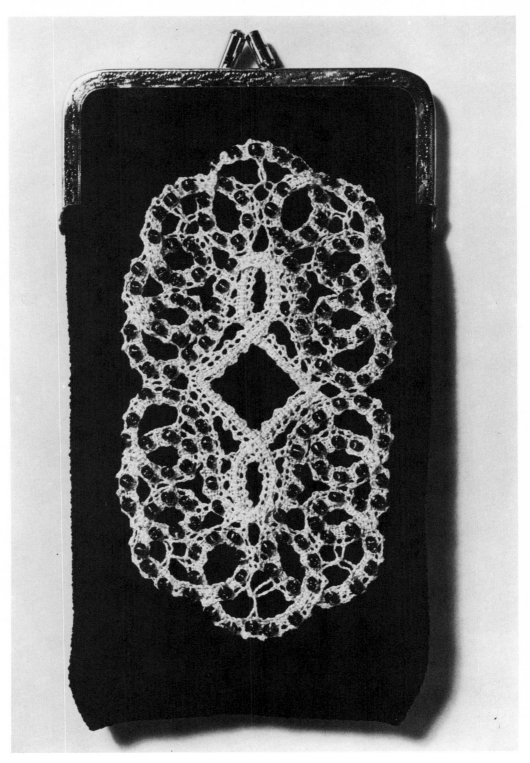

206 *Valentine*

True-love-knot

Valentine design

Illustrations **206**, **207** and **208** trace the development of a design idea. The original idea came from a magazine article on valentine cards. A tracing of one of the illustrations – an eighteenth century, hand-painted card – provided the pricking for **206**. Basic braid with a central cable was worked on this using 8 pairs of machine twist (including 1 contrast thread for the cable). Various fillings were worked with pairs 'sewn' to the edge of the braid.

Book cover

The next stage was to redraw the design, at about twice the size, on squared paper. The book cover design in **207** was worked on this using 9 pairs No 8 cotton perle. The braid is whole stitch with two lines of cording giving contrast spots (**108**) and a second contrast pair worked in doubles on the left hand edge.

This square when part worked showed up a possible use as the decoration for a cloth so the pattern was further adapted to give a linkage between two heart motifs.

Pricking **209** can be used for either a cloth or the book cover. For the book cover use just the two hearts and two small squares, tracing them twice to give the full square motif. Follow A to J of the

207 Book cover

117

order of work given below for the tray cloth – note
that no long loop (F) will be needed on the edge of
the heart.

Tray cloth

Use the whole of pricking **209**, with extra hearts
traced for the long sides, and 9 pairs No 8 cotton
perle: 7 prs main colour; 2 prs contrast. Work in
basic braid using one contrast pair and one main
colour for the central chain (see **109**), and the other
contrasts as the left-hand edge pair. Start at A.

Work the small square making corners as in
166b, with at least one of the turning stitches on
the outside of the central chain – this prevents
crowding of the spots. At B twist the contrast edge
pair 6 times, 'sew' to C and twist 6 times more. At
D twist workers 16 times and take round a pin at
E. At F twist workers 6 times and take round a pin
at G. At H plait workers and edge pairs (make
picots if desired), take round the pin at E, make a
'sewing' to the start of the plait at H.

Make a 'sewing' at I and at all other points
where two parts of the braid touch or cross. Where
the braid crosses itself the 'sewing' can be made
with the edge pair instead of the workers. At J
twist workers 8 times, 'sew' through plaited and
twisted loops at E, twist 8 times. At K twist edge
pair 6 times, 'sew' to L, twist 6 times, take round a
pin at M, twist 6 times. At N twist workers 6 times,
'sew' to O, twist 6 times.

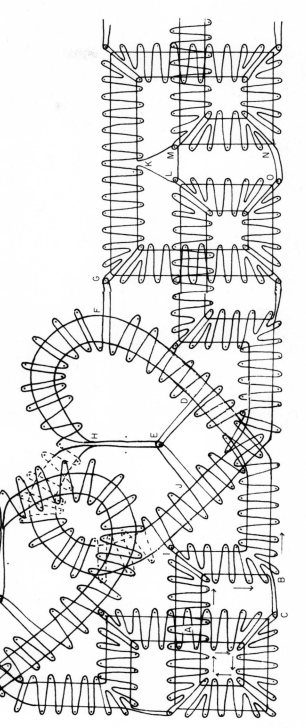

Letters

Lettering can provide great scope for experiment whether for individual initials, monograms or complete words. The style of lettering will dictate the type of braid to be used. Two styles are illustrated here – straightforward capitals for the word 'BRAIDS' (above) and more ornate initials, based on Celtic designs, for the pendants (on pages 122 and 123). Other ideas for letter shapes could be taken from alphabets designed for other crafts – embroidery for example, or stone masonry. Elaborate fillings of plaits and tallies could be used where appropriate, or simple fillings of twisted threads as in the 'b' pendant. Working the letter face down will allow joins to be made on the wrong side – trace the pattern then reverse onto plain paper for this. Widening the foot of a letter into a serif (see 'R' pendant) will reduce bulkiness caused by the darning in of ends.

Applications

Letters of the size illustrated here can be applied to a wide range of items: household linen, purses, tabards, bookcovers are just a few examples. Smaller letters worked in fine thread, such as machine embroidery thread, will add individuality to handkerchiefs or other small items. In many cases the letter can complement an edging, or even be worked into a braid border – on the corner of a waistcoat for example.

Letters worked on a much larger scale give a new range of applications. Work in thick wools, twine or cord (possibly with a thinner thread for the workers) and use the letters as bold motifs on bags, ponchos etc, or even glued to a child's bedroom door.

Working methods

Care must be taken with where and how the braid is started and finished. Most letters will be started as in **T8**, but any of the finishing methods given on page 89 can be used – for example 'B' opposite has ends darned in while 'I' is finished with a tuft. Ends can also be tied in pairs, cut off close and finished with a spot of glue.

Formal letters

Two colours – gold (No 8 cotton perle) and white (No 60 crochet cotton) – were used for each of the letters (**210**) which were worked as follows.

For the letter 'B', use 10 pairs (5 gold, 5 white). Braid **80a**, without a row of doubles on the inside edge, is worked with gold threads on the outside, white inside. Start and finish at *a–b* (**211**). Note that there are more rows of gold than white on corners and curves; and that the white is worked alone from *c* to *d*, with 3 'sewings' to the upright and one to itself.

211 Working diagrams for 'BRAIDS'

For the letter 'R', use 8 pairs (each pair 1 white and 1 gold thread). The letter is in three sections: *a* to *b* is worked as **106a**; 6 pairs are then 'sewn' to *c* and worked round to *d* as in **106b**; finally 8 pairs are 'sewn' at *e* for **106a** again.

For the letter 'A', use 14 pairs (8 white, 6 gold). Each side of the letter is braid **74** worked with 7 pairs. Start at *a*, with 2 gold and 4 white pairs laid across the top pin (see **161**), the remaining pairs added between *a* and *b*, and the two braids worked together as far as *c*. The tally is worked between *d* and *e* with the two pairs of workers. This could be worked as one braid (7 pairs) starting at *y* and finishing at *z*. A different method of working *d* to *e* would then be needed, for example a double plait.

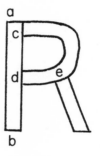

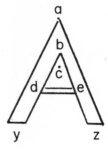

For the letter 'I', use 8 pairs (7 white plus 1 gold for the gimp). Braid **90** is used, with small beads added using a crochet hook (**T15b**).

For the letter 'D', use 7 pairs (4 gold, 3 white). Use braid **86b**, starting at the bottom of the upright.

For the letter 'S', use 11 pairs (10 white, 1 gold). Braid **109** is used, with closed edges. The gold pair is linked with one of the white at the start of the chain to prevent unravelling. The edge pairs are twisted 1, 2 or 3 times between pins.

Letter pendants

Each of the pendants illustrated in **212** has a braid letter mounted (using transparent glue) on a shaped piece of acrylic sheet. For the 'R' pendant (**212a**) a half stitch braid changing to tenstick then back to half stitch is worked with 6 pairs of machine twist. The shape of the motif can be formed on the pricking, but most of the interweaving of the braid must be worked when the letter has been removed from the pillow.

For the 'J' pendant (**212b**), braid **86b** is worked with 4 pairs cotton perle and 3 pairs lurex. Start at the tip of the lower loop. Short cross piece: whole stitch worked with one lurex pair and the two passive pairs from one side of the braid, 'sewings' are made as the braid returns to the centre.

For the 'b' pendant (**212c**), use 7 pairs: 4 pairs dark for a whole stitch braid – with picots on the outer edge for part of the length – and 3 pairs light for braid **126a**. Both braids started as four strand plaits worked in small circles before adding the extra pairs. W st/pin/w st links the two braids. The filling is made with pairs discarded from the light braid, twisted and taken across the inside of the letter. By the end of the loop the one remaining light pair is worked in w st with the darker braid.

212 *Pendants*

a

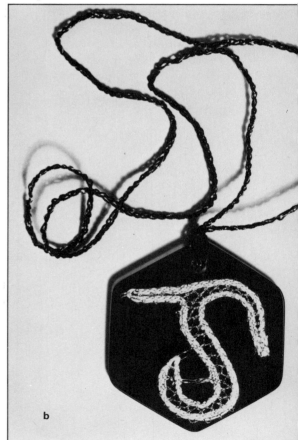

b

The first three pendants are suspended on crocheted chains.

For the 'G' pendant (212d), braid 109 is worked with 6 pairs black machine twist and 1 pair silver embroidery thread. The pendant is suspended on a chain worked on pricking 213 (part a) using 2 pairs silver and 2 pairs No 8 black cotton perle. The path of each pair is shown, doubles are worked where two pairs cross, and small beads are added using T25b. Part b of pricking 213 is used for the braid that surrounds the mount, this has a gimp on each side which, when pulled up slightly, will enclose the edge of the acrylic shape.

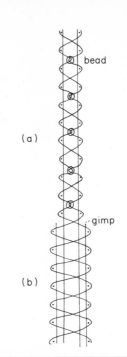

(a)

bead

gimp

(b)

213 Pricking for pendant chain

c

d

214 Bird

Animal motifs

Bird

Use pricking **215** for the bird in **214**. This example was worked with thrums from a ropeworks – about the thickness of machine embroidery thread. For the outline, use 9 pairs, and work basic braid with a closed outside edge. Start at the end of the upper tail feather. Finish on the lower feather with the threads tied together and cut off as a short tassel.

For the body filling, work Torchon ground, with a square tally worked into the ground for the eye. Start at the head, 'sewing' threads to the outline where needed. When the diagonal X—Y has been worked, turn the pillow and work along the body.

For the extra tail feathers, work one braid in whole stitch, and one in whole stitch with doubles along one edge. Work one with threads continued from the ground, the other with threads 'sewn' in or added as in T22. Make 'sewings' between feathers.

Work the wing shape separately in tenstick using 6 pairs, then sew to the body.

215 Pricking for bird

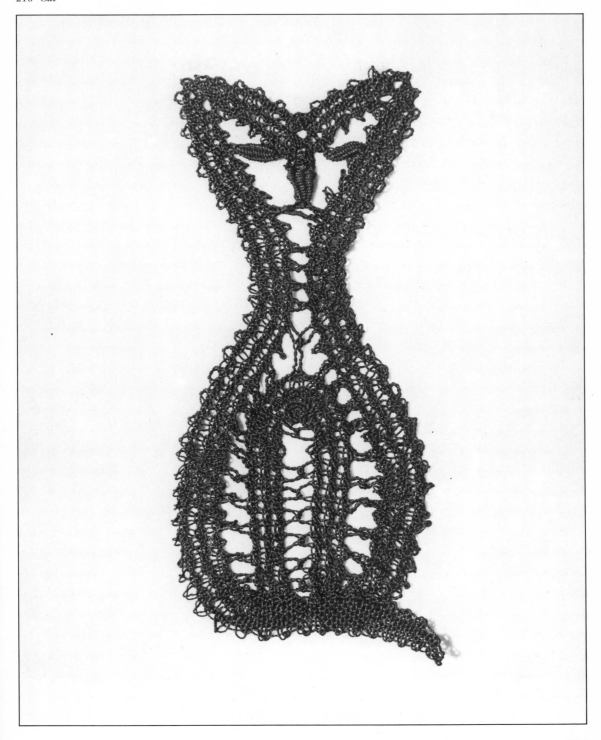

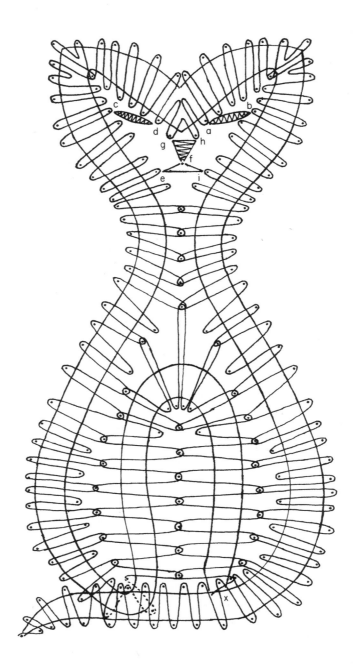

Cat

Use pricking **217** for the cat design in **216**, and 7 pairs No 12 cotton perle. Work the motif face down on the pillow. Start at the tip of the tail with three pairs, and add one extra pair on each of the first four rows (see **158**). Work whole stitch for the tail. Work the body and head in whole stitch also, but between rows bring the passives together with doubles – 1st and 2nd pairs and 5th and 6th after the first row, 3rd and 4th after the next (**218**). Twist the workers twice or more at the pins. Make 'sewings' where necessary.

218 *Arrangements of stitches for working cat*

For the eyes, use 2 prs from the edge at *a* to make a leaf shaped tally. 'Sew' to *b*, treating the four threads as one pair. Plait the threads loosely to take them back across the tally to *a*, 'sew' to the start of the tally. Work the second eye between *c* and *d*. For the mouth and nose, plait from *e* to *f*; make a triangular tally, 'sew' 1 pr to *g*, 1 pr to *h*; plait across tally; 'sew' to *f*; plait to *i*; 'sew'; plait back to *e*, 'sew'. Finish at X.

Mouse

Use pricking **220** for the mouse in **219**, 10 pairs machine twist in two shades (5 prs each shade), and a small black bead. To start, hang the 5 darker pairs across the pin at A; work two or three rows in half stitch (no doubles on the edge). Hang the remaining threads at B, work several rows of this lighter braid – also half stitch – making a 'sewing' to the dark braid at A.

For the body, work each braid in turn round the other, making 'sewings' at shared pinholes. Turning stitches, where required between 'sewings', are half stitch. To make the tail, work the darker braid in whole stitch once it leaves the body. Discard two pairs towards the tip. Knot the remaining three pairs and cut off as a tassel.

For the head; continue in half stitch with the lighter braid. Use T15b to apply the small bead at C for the eye. Make turning stitches on the inside of the nose at D. 'Sew' each pair to the body between E and F, and carefully darn in the ends. To make the ear, 'sew' four pairs at G to work a tenstick braid to H.

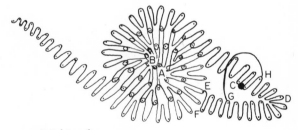

220 *Pricking for mouse*

219 *Mouse*

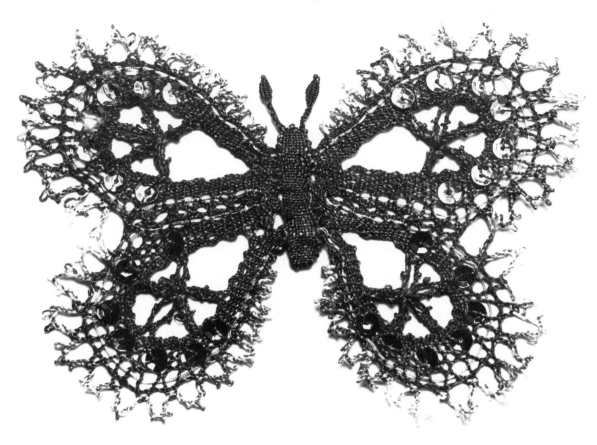

Butterfly

Use pricking **222** for the design in **221**. The butterfly motif uses many of the techniques described in the earlier chapters. The example illustrated was worked with home-dyed linen thread, but any fairly fine thread could be used (eg No 60 crochet cotton). Use the following materials: 9 pairs (7 prs dark purple; 2 prs light purple – for the plaited edge); 1 gimp composed of 2 thicknesses of silver cording; 28 sequins.

The motif is worked face down on the pillow. Wind bobbins in pairs (T8). With 2 pairs pinned at A: work a leaf of 8 weavings (T14), then a plait of 3 doubles (T2). Do the same with 2 pairs pinned at B. Pin 2 more pairs at C. Work the body in whole stitch, taking the two right-hand bobbins as workers (T5).

At the tail, tie the workers tightly round the other threads. Take all the threads back along the body, 'sew' one pair to 1 and a second pair to 2 (T19). Tie this pair round the rest of the threads (**223**). Attach a gimp to lie between the pair from 1 and the rest of the threads (T12).

Proceed with the half stitch braid, including the gimp, until the pin is stuck at 10 (T7). Hang an extra pair over the pin at 8, work this into the braid (T22). 'Sew' the last two pairs to 9 for the plaited edge with picots (T10). Work 1, $1\frac{1}{2}$ or 2 doubles between the picots.

After putting in the pin at 16, plait the two inside pairs, making picots at 17 and 19 and taking the plait round a pin at 18 (T24b). 'Sew' the plait to 16 and continue with the half stitch braid. Use a fine crochet hook to apply sequins on every fourth

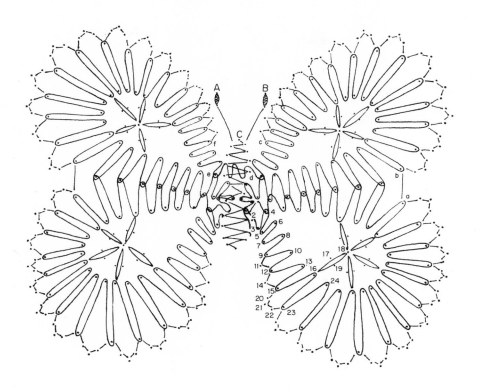

row of the wider part of the wing (T15b). Take four plaits round the pin at 18, 'sew' the fifth plait into all four loops.

After *a* leave the edge plait on one side, pick it up again when the workers reach *b*. Make 'sewings' at 2 and 4. Curve the braid with turning stitches; 'sew' to the edge of the body (T20). Connect the upper to the lower wing with seven 'sewings'.

At *c*, leave the plait and discard one other pair of threads, later tie and cut off these threads (T23). 'Sew' the workers to the body at *d*. Work two rows of braid (without pins) to cross the body. 'Sew' the workers to *e*. Complete the second side to match the first, rejoining three pairs at *f*. At the finish, 'sew' the threads to the body before knotting and cutting off.

223 *Working the butterfly tail*

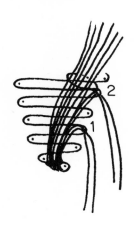

Abbreviations

pr(s) – pair(s), ie two threads or two bobbins

wks – workers

tw – twist, ie right thread of a pair over left

cr – cross, ie left thread of one pair over right
   thread of next pair

$\frac{1}{2}$ st – half stitch: tw/cr

w st – whole stitch: cr/tw/cr

dbl – double: tw/cr/tw/cr

Glossary

basic braid – braid consisting of a central panel of whole stitch with edge pairs worked in doubles.

bobbins – handles that carry the working threads.

chain – two lines of cording worked together.

cording – line formed by passing workers between two contrast threads on every row.

cross – left thread of one pair over right thread of neighbouring pair.

crossing – exchange of position of two or more pairs of thread.

double – tw/cr/tw/cr.

edge pair – pair of threads at the side of the braid, may run the length of the braid or change places with the workers.

edging – braid or lace designed to be attached by one edge only. The term may apply to the whole braid or to part.

filling – an arrangement of tallies, plaits or twisted threads crossing a space in a fabric.

gimp – a single thick thread held in place by passing between two other threads.

ground – a regular arrangement of stitches within a piece of lace.

half stitch – tw/cr.

passive – thread running along the length of the braid.

picot – an ornamental loop.

pillow – base on which the braid is worked.

pricker – tool for making holes in card pricking.

pricking – pattern marked on card or paper and including pinholes.

row – once across the braid: from left to right *or* right to left.

'sewing' – use of crochet hook to connect two braids, or parts of braids.

tally – small solid block formed by weaving one thread backwards and forwards between three others.

Torchon – a geometric form of lace.

turning stitch – the last stitch of a row where there is no pin.

twist – right thread of a pair over the left.

weaving – making tallies: one weaving takes one thread over and under three others from right to left *and* from left to right.

whole stitch – cr/tw/cr.

workers – pair of threads passing from side to side of the braid.

Appendix

224 Framework for French pillow

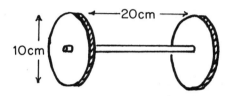

Making a French pillow

This is a more permanent form of the cylindrical pillow described in chapter 1. It consists of a roller let into the centre of a padded pillow. Make sturdy wooden frames to the dimensions given in **224**. Cover with suitable material nailed (preferably with upholstery nails) to the edges marked with crosshatching. Stuff the base with kapok to produce a smooth, firm surface. Stuff the roller with bran or sawdust, packing very tightly. Use a small wedge (eg half a peg) to hold the roller firmly in the base (**225**).

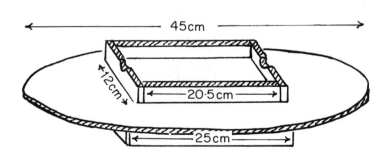

225 Completed French pillow

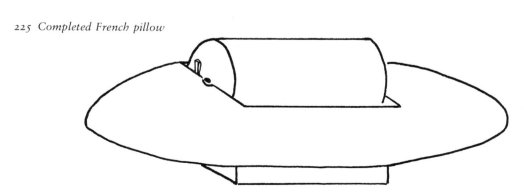

This pillow is ideal for lengths of braid or lace but is inconvenient for working corners or motifs. For these the pillow can be adapted by replacing the roller with a block of polystyrene packaging material (cut to fit flush with the padded surface) covered with one or two layers of fabric.

Old bobbins and pillows
Old – even antique – bobbins are usually improved by use, providing any obvious damage (such as loose pewter ornament) is made good. Old pillows may be quite soft, especially in the middle, and need restuffing; all should be provided with a new (washable) cover.

Threads
The standard range of crochet cottons, cotton perle, etc, can be obtained from needlework and craft shops (or departments of large stores). Haberdashery departments provide machine twist, thicker thread (intended for top stitching) and shirring elastic. Knitting wool is readily available from many outlets. Look out for the more unusual threads: for example on market stalls for carpet thrums etc, in garden or fishing shops for various twines.

Beads
Beads can be found in craft and toy shops or departments, also in jumble sales, charity shops, etc, in the form of beaded work or old necklaces.

Pricking film
Architect's tracing film (*Carbelon*) can be bought by the metre (yard) from some office stationers. An alternative to this film is the transparent material used for overhead projectors; this is rather tougher than *Carbelon*, and has the disadvantage that the special pen required to write on the surface is not suitable for fine lines or accurate dots.

Lace classes in the UK
Evening (or afternoon) classes are held in many Adult Education centres throughout the country – enquire at your local library. Weekend, or longer, courses are also arranged both for beginners and more advanced students, details of these can be obtained through the Lace Guild.

The Lace Guild is one of two organisations formed in the United Kingdom during recent years to revive the art of lace making. It now has an international membership and publishes a quarterly magazine, *Lace*, which contains articles on all types of lace in addition to information on classes and residential courses. The Guild can be contacted through the Federation of British Craft Societies at 43 Earlham Street, London WC2H 9LD.

The other organisation is the Lace Society which concentrates on bobbin lace in its quarterly newsletter. The Society can be contacted through the Craft Advisory Committee, 12 Waterloo Place, London SW1Y 4AU.

Suppliers of Equipment and Materials

Lacemaking equipment can be obtained by post from the following:

UK

Mrs A Sells
Lane Cove
49 Pedley Lane
Clifton
Shefford
Bedfordshire

Equipment, threads and books

D J Hornsby (Woodturner)
149 High Street
Burton Latimer
Kettering
Northamptonshire

Bobbins, bobbin winders, equipment

Mace & Nairn
89 Crane Street
Salisbury
Wiltshire SP1 2PY

Threads and equipment

The Needlewoman Shop
146 Regent Street
London W1

Thread, pins, bobbins

De Denne Ltd
159/161 Kenton Road
Kenton
Harrow
Middlesex

Threads and beads

Creative Beadcraft Ltd
Unit 26, Chiltern Trading Estate
Earl Howe Road
Holmer Green
High Wycombe
Buckinghamshire

Beads and sequins

USA

Berga-Ullman, inc.
P.O. Box 918
North Adams, Massachusetts
01247
All supplies

Frederick J. Fawcett Inc.
129 South Street
Boston
Mass 02111
Linen yarns

Osma Galliger Tod Studio
319 Mendoza Avenue
Coral Gables
Florida 33134
Yarns, bobbins, cushions

Robin and Russ Handweavers
533 N. Adams Street
McMinnville, Oregon 97128
Books, materials and equipment

Some Place
2990 Adeline Street
Berkeley
California 94703
Yarns, bobbins, cushions

Textile Studios, Inc.
Windsor Mill
121 Union Street
North Adams, Massachusetts
01247
Large selection of metallic and silk threads

The Unique and Art Lace
Cleaners
5926 Delmar Boulevard
St. Louis, Missouri 63112
Professional lace cleaning and restoration

Bibliography

This is by no means a comprehensive list: in recent years several old lace books have been reprinted and new ones published. Out of print books are often obtainable through the local library. Patterns may be found in general needlework books, old magazines or foreign language publications.

Terms vary: for example, what is called 'whole stitch' in this book in another might be called 'cloth stitch' or 'linen weave', while 'doubles' are called 'whole stitch'. Another difference that may be disconcerting is in the instructions for half stitch: in some books the order of movements is given as cross/twist. This makes no difference to the finished work providing the pairs are given the correct number of twists at the beginning and end of a half stitch piece.

UK

KLIOT, K. and J., *Bobbin Lace: Form by the Twisting of Cords* (Allen & Unwin, London, 1974; Crown Publishers Inc, New York, 1973)
A modern look at the use of bobbins. Step by step photographs of various techniques and traditional stitches, plus ideas for experimental work.

LUXTON, E., *The Technique of Honiton Lace* (Batsford, London, 1979; Charles T. Branford Co, Boston, 1979)
A complete guide to the making of fine Honiton lace.

MINCOFF, E. and MARRIAGE, M., *Pillow Lace: A Practical Manual* (First published 1907; reprinted Paul Minet, London, 1971)
History, techniques and fifty patterns with directions and full scale prickings.

MAIDMENT, M., *A Manual of Handmade Bobbin Lace Work* (Charles T. Branford Co, Boston, 1931; reprinted Piccadilly Rare Books, Paul Minet, London, 1971)
A textbook for the working of all types of traditional bobbin lace. Few complete prickings, but a good basis for composing your own patterns.

NOTTINGHAM, P., *The Technique of Bobbin Lace* (Batsford, London, 1976; Van Nostrand Reinhold Co, New York, 1976)
Excellent instructions, prickings and working diagrams for an attractive collection of Torchon, Bedfordshire and Buckinghamshire lace.

NOTTINGHAM, P., *The Technique of Torchon Lace* (Batsford, 1979)
Techniques and patterns for Torchon edgings, collars, corners and mats.

USA

In the United States, the society of the *International Old Lacers* publishes bulletins for its members six times a year.

BATH, Virginia Churchill, *Lace* (Regnery, Chicago, 1974)

FUHRMANN, Brigita, *Bobbin Lace: A Contemporary Approach* (Watson-Guptill Publications, New York, 1976)

GUBSER, Elsie H., *Bobbin Lace* (Robin & Russ Handweavers, Oregon, 1975)

JACKSON, Emily F., *A History of Handmade Lace* (Charles Scribner's Sons, New York, 1900)

KELLOGG, Charlotte, *Bobbins of Belgium* (Funk & Wagnalls Co, 1920)

MAY, Florence Lewis, *Hispanic Lace and Lace Making* (Hispanic Society of America, 1939)

POND, Gabrielle, *An Introduction to Lace* (Charles Scribner's Sons, New York, 1973)

SHARP, Mary, *Point and Pillow Lace* (E. P. Dutton & Co, New York, 1913)

TOD, Osma G., *The Belgian Way of Making Bobbin Lace* (O. G. Tod Studio, Florida)

TOD, Osma G., *Bobbin Lace Step by Step* (O. G. Tod Studio, Florida, 1969)

WHITING, Gertrude, *A Lace Guide for Makers and Collectors* (E. P. Dutton & Co, New York, 1920)

Index

Abbreviations 130
  as instructions 21
Acrylic sheet 122
Adding threads 89
Animal motifs 122ff
Angles 57, 90
Angled braid 57
  linked 104
  plaited 69
Antique bobbins 11, 133
Architect's tracing film 34, 133

Bag, lavender 104
  shoulder 112
Basic braid 22ff
  looped 52
Beads 31ff
  applied by 'sewings' 95
  belt 101
  edging 71
  motif 114
  sources 133
Belts 101f
Bird 124
Bobbins 10, 133
  replacing empty 20
  winding 13
  wound in pairs 19
Bobble 31
Book cover 117
Bookmark 106
'BRAIDS' 120
Braids, basic 22ff
  simple 21
  with two or more worker pairs 42ff
Butterfly motif 128
  thread 96

Cable, see cording
Cat 125ff

Chain cording 27
  spots 60
  zigzag 62
Chain, crochet for pendants 123
  crochet to join braids 94
Celtic designs 122f
Changing prickings 93
  pairing of threads 96
Clasp, fixing threads to 87
Classes 133
Closed edge 23f
Cording 26
  spots 60
Corner for waved braid 54
  Torchon 81
  see also Angles
Cover cloth 20, 93
Crochet cotton 12
  hook – see Hook
Cross 14
Crossing gimps 25
  3 or 4 pairs 37f
  whole stitch braids 66, 79
Curves 90

Darning 89
Designing prickings 97
  for letters 120
  from valentine 116
Diamonds 80f
Discarding threads 89
Doubles 18
  braid 21
    waved 54
  ground 76
  edge for half stitch 21
Dowelling for bobbins 10
Dress yoke, baby's 110
  trimming 98
Dyeing threads 96

Edge pair 22
  closed 27f
Edgings 71
  scalloped 72
  with plaits and tallies 38ff
Elastic belt 102
  thread 96
Equipment 9ff
Evening purse 114
Experimenting 97

Fan 84ff
Fillings 93
Film, tracing 133
Finger weaving 70f
  as bag handle 113
Finishing 89
Flat pillow, to make 10
  use of 20, 93
Flower 98
Fragile braid 64
French pillow 132
Fringe braid 36
  finish 89
  on poncho 108
  start 87
Finishing 89

Gimp 25
  in Torchon ground 74ff

Hairpin waved braid 54
Half stitch 18
  bookmark 106
  braid 21
  diamond 81
  edging 72
  ground 74
  ovals 48
Handkerchief corner 99
Heart motif 116ff
Holes 24
  in Torchon ground 78
Hook, applying beads with 31, 95
  for 'sewings' 51
Honiton lace 69

Jar 105

Joining braids 95
  ends 89

Lace 7
  Honiton 69
  Torchon 74ff
Lace Guild 133
Ladder braid 24
  rings 50
  with surface contrasts 61
Large designs 97
Lavender bag 104
Leaf tally 28f
Le Pompe 67
Lettering 120ff
Linked braids 43, 63
  angled braids 104
Looped braids 52
Loops, eliminating 19

Metallic thread 96
Motifs 98f
Mounting 96
Mouse 127
Moving braid on pillow 20

Open braids 42f
  used as a belt 102
Origins of lace 7
Oval, half stitch 48
  holes 79
  whole stitch with tallies 65

Pairs 14
  bobbins wound in 19
Paperweight 105
Passives 17, 22
Patterns – *see* Prickings
Pendants 122f
Picot 23f
  on plaits 38f
Pillow 9f
  French 132
  setting up 16
  use of flat 20, 93
Pillow lace 7
Pins 12, 19
Plait 14f

as belt 101
as edging 38ff
surface 61
Plait and picot braid 66
filling 99
scalloped edging 72
Plait and tally edging 38
Plaited angled braids 68
Poncho 108
Pricker 12
Prickings 12
designing 97
for curves and angles 90
preparing 15, 34
(see also instructions for individual braids and
motifs)
Purse 114

Quatrefoil 100

Rectangular tally 28
in ground 76f
Rings 50
whole stitch 66
as tie motif 103
Row 17
of basic braid 22

Sampler, as bookmark 106
fan 85f
tally 30
whole stitch – double – half stitch 18
Scalloped edgings 72
Sequins, applying 31
on motifs 105, 128
Serpentine braid 54
Setting up 16
'Sewings' 51f
to add beads 95
to add threads 88
Shaping 87, 90
Shoulder bag 113
Spider 82ff
braid for shoulder bag 113
Spots 60
Star 105
Starting 16, 87
two braids together 88, 103
with bobbins wound in pairs 19

Stitch, double 18
half 19
whole 17
Stretch belt 102
Stretchy thread 96
Stripes 58f
Surface contrasts 61
tallies 28

Tally 27f
features 124ff
filling 100
in Torchon ground 76f, 113
surface 28
Tenstick 69
for paperweight 105
Tapered start 87
Threads 12, 96
Three colour edging 73
Thrums, carpet 71, 113
ropemaker's 64
Tie 103
Torchon 74ff
bookmark 106
filling 124
shoulder bag 112
Tray cloth 118
Trefoil, tenstick 69
basic braid 99
Trimmings 98
True-love-knot 116f
Turning stitch 53, 69
Twist 14
Twisted threads as fillings 98

Valentine 116
Variations 23

Waved braids 54f
for poncho 108
Weaving, finger 70
tallies 28
Whole stitch 17
braid 21
looped 52
diamond 81
ground 84
rings 67
as tie motif 103

Workers 17, 22
  path of 35
  two pairs 43

Yoke, baby's dress 110
  edging 98

Zigzag chain braid 62
  on dress yoke 110